THE YOUNG ADULT'S GUIDE TO SCHOOL FUNDRAISING

101 Fun & Easy Ideas for
Small Events

By Lisa McGinnes

THE YOUNG ADULT'S GUIDE TO SCHOOL FUNDRAISING: 101 FUN & EASY IDEAS FOR SMALL EVENTS

1405 SW 6th Avenue • Ocala, Florida 34471 • Phone 800-814-1132 • Fax 352-622-1875
Website: www.atlantic-pub.com • Email: sales@atlantic-pub.com
SAN Number: 268-1250

Library of Congress Cataloging-in-Publication Data

Names: McGinnes, Lisa, author.
Title: School fundraising 101 : fun & easy ideas for small events / Lisa McGinnes.
Description: Ocala, Florida : Atlantic Publishing Group, Inc, [2017] | Includes bibliographical references.
Identifiers: LCCN 2017051429 (print) | LCCN 2017054231 (ebook) | ISBN 9781620231647 (ebook) | ISBN 9781620231630 (pbk. : alk. paper) | ISBN 1620231638 (alk. paper) | ISBN 9781620232323 (hardcover)
Subjects: LCSH: Fund raising. | Educational fund raising.
Classification: LCC HV41.2 (ebook) | LCC HV41.2 .M4165 2017 (print) | DDC 371.2/06—dc23
LC record available at https://lccn.loc.gov/2017051429

Printed in the United States

PROJECT MANAGER: Danielle Lieneman
INTERIOR LAYOUT AND JACKET DESIGN: Nicole Sturk

Reduce. Reuse.
RECYCLE.

A decade ago, Atlantic Publishing signed the Green Press Initiative. These guidelines promote environmentally friendly practices, such as using recycled stock and vegetable-based inks, avoiding waste, choosing energy-efficient resources, and promoting a no-pulping policy. We now use 100-percent recycled stock on all our books. The results: in one year, switching to post-consumer recycled stock saved 24 mature trees, 5,000 gallons of water, the equivalent of the total energy used for one home in a year, and the equivalent of the greenhouse gases from one car driven for a year.

Over the years, we have adopted a number of dogs from rescues and shelters. First there was Bear and after he passed, Ginger and Scout. Now, we have Kira, another rescue. They have brought immense joy and love not just into our lives, but into the lives of all who met them.

We want you to know a portion of the profits of this book will be donated in Bear, Ginger and Scout's memory to local animal shelters, parks, conservation organizations, and other individuals and nonprofit organizations in need of assistance.

– Douglas & Sherri Brown,
President & Vice-President of Atlantic Publishing

Table of Contents

Food and Drinks

Games and Contests

Holidays and Special Occasions

Shows

Sports

Themed Events

Sales

Miscellaneous

Introduction

If you belong to any organization, you know there is always a need to raise money — for the dance squad to attend an out-of-state competition, the orchestra to purchase new instruments, the drama club to rent costumes, or the soccer team to buy equipment.

Whether you need to raise funds for your school group, sports team, church, or any other group or nonprofit organization, you will find your next small fundraising event here.

Each event has a description so you can determine which ones meet your financial capabilities and suit your social objectives. The estimated cost for putting on the event is represented by up to five dollar signs — $ is the lowest cost involved and $$$$$ is the highest cost.

Events take a certain amount of effort to organize. Each event listing is rated one to five stars for obtaining sponsorship, finding a venue, recruiting volunteers, preparation, and execution. Again, one is the lowest amount of difficulty and five is the most difficult.

Any special equipment or materials are listed, along with ideas for sponsors, donations, venues, and how many volunteers will be needed.

You'll also find web resources for more information and success stories to give you an idea of how other groups have been successful with that event.

Not everyone is comfortable with selling something or asking people for money. This book gives you lots of ideas for fundraisers that will fit your group's dynamic and help you to be successful, so you can get the cash you need and get on with your life. Remember to be sincere — most people in the community want to help young people succeed, but they won't know what you need unless you ask. It helps to have a specific goal in mind, but don't forget to have fun! Good luck with your fundraising event.

Rationale behind the ratings

★	The fundraiser is very easy or costs little to nothing.
★ ★	While still easy to do, events with this ranking need slightly more work, planning, or money to pull off.
★ ★ ★	A moderate amount of work or money is necessary. You may have to find volunteers who are willing and able to sell somewhat expensive products or tickets. You may have to book a venue, which is at least moderately challenging.
★ ★ ★ ★	There is more than the average amount of time, effort, or funds required.
★ ★ ★ ★ ★	The event is somewhat difficult or expensive. It may require a lot of preparation or hands-on work. It may require a lot of materials or resources.

Arts and Crafts

1. Community Mural Project

What better way to get attention for your cause than a larger-than-life art display?

Description: Invite the community to create a colorful mural using various media — it's a great way to get attention for your cause and get people excited about it. Charge an entry fee, and either display the finished artwork or auction it off to raise additional funds.

Estimated Cost:

Levels of Difficulty:

Obtaining Sponsors/Donations	★ ★ ★
Finding a Venue	★ ★ ★ ★
Recruiting Volunteers	★ ★ ★
Preparation	★ ★ ★ ★ ★
Execution	★ ★ ★

Special Materials/Equipment:

☐ Art materials (such as paint, pencils, and brushes)

Sponsors/Donations:

- Contact an art supply, home improvement, or superstore for donations of art materials.

- *Tip:* Stores like Walmart and Lowe's will often donate a gift card if you ask the local manager.

Possible Venue(s): Community or church meeting facilities, public parks (for an art-in-the-park event), sports arenas, or playing fields work well.

Tip: If you have space at your school, this can be a great way to publicize your cause.

Recommended Volunteers: 10+ to create and install the mural

Preparation: Talk to your school administrators or local business owners to find out whether they would be interested in having a community mural installed on a wall inside or outside of their building. Have a local artist draw a sketch, then cut it into six-inch squares that participants can work on. Promote the event on social media and through local newspapers, magazines, and radio stations. Stress that no previous art experience is necessary. Recommend that participants bring their own art materials, if possible.

Execution: Charge an entry fee to participate in the project. Allow participants to choose the section they wish to work on using their choice of art materials, and try to accommodate families or groups that want to work together on a larger section. Assemble the completed sections into the finished art project that can be displayed, and hopefully auctioned off to raise even more money.

Tip(s):

- Ask a local artist to donate his or her services to oversee construction of the project.

- Choose a theme for the mural to give it cohesiveness — preferably one that draws attention to your cause.

- If the finished artwork will be displayed outside, choose waterproof and wind-resistant media.

Variation(s):

- Create a tile mosaic community project using donated materials.

2. Custom Art Memory Books/Photo Books

Give parents a better way to save their children's art than on the fridge!

Description: Take orders from parents at the start of the school year to create memory books of the art their children made at school throughout the year. You can either create custom scrapbooks using the actual art, or you can photograph the best pieces and use them to make an attractive photo album.

Estimated Cost:

Levels of Difficulty:

Obtaining Sponsors/Donations	★★★★★
Finding a Venue	★★
Recruiting Volunteers	★★★
Preparation	★★★★★
Execution	★★★★★

Special Materials/Equipment:

- ☐ One scrapbook or photo album per order (preferably in school colors)

- ☐ Other scrapbooking paraphernalia (including page embellishments, decorative stamps, stencils, and adhesives)

Sponsors/Donations:

- Art, craft, and scrapbooking stores may be willing to donate clearance and past-season merchandise.

- Ask retail stores for cash donations to cover the cost of the scrapbooks or photo albums.

Possible Venue(s): Preschools and elementary schools are best, but it may also be possible to interest a high school art department in a high-end product.

Recommended Volunteers: 12+ depending on the number of orders you secure. If you have experienced "scrappers" among your members, be sure to recruit them to help. A volunteer who is good with a digital camera may also be needed.

Preparation: Create an email to send to parents at the beginning of the school year to advertise the product. Add a shopping cart to your website so parents can place orders online. Create original page layouts. If you are photographing the art, schedule with the teachers when you can come in and take photos before projects are graded and sent home.

Execution: If you choose to collect the actual art, as projects are completed throughout the year, collect them for inclusion in each child's memory book. If you choose to photograph the art, watch for sales on easy-to-use websites that will allow you to upload pictures and easily customize photo books. Shutterfly.com has a special deal for school fundraisers.

Tip(s):

- Put the child's photograph on the cover. Parents love seeing photos of their children.

- Let the children make a dedication page.

Variation(s):

- Take orders from parents at the start of the school year to create books of the writing (essays, poetry, short stories, reports) their children did at school throughout the year.

Web resource(s):

www.shutterfly.com/fundraising

3. Family Portraits/Photo Booth

Because parents and grandparents are always looking for affordable, unique family portraits!

Description: Find a talented student photographer who can take family portraits, or contact the company that takes your school's pictures to see if you can get a special deal. Sell enlarged and matted portraits, photo print packages, or edited images the family can print themselves.

Estimated Cost:

Levels of Difficulty:

Obtaining Sponsors/Donations	★ ★ ★ ★ ★
Finding a Venue	★ ★ ★
Recruiting Volunteers	★ ★ ★
Preparation	★ ★ ★ ★
Execution	★ ★

Special Materials/Equipment:

☐ Attractive backdrop or outdoor setting

☐ Digital photography equipment

☐ Chairs or benches, and props

Sponsors/Donations:

• Contact a creative arts school or studio to find a student photographer who might donate his or her services.

- Ask a photo studio for permission to borrow a photo backdrop, or for permission to use studio space during off hours; or ask a photo booth rental company to donate their services. Consider raising funds to have the digital pictures printed and matted.

Possible Venue(s): A photo, dance, or music studio with neutral-colored walls, or an uncluttered community or church meeting facility works well for well-lit, inside photos. Many photographers now prefer doing these shoots outside, so a park can be a great space and evening light is usually optimal.

Recommended Volunteers: 4-5 to set up backdrops, take photos, and keep track of orders

Preparation: Promote the portrait sale on social media, in notices in church and school newsletters, flyers on vehicles, and notices on public bulletin boards. Add a notice about the event to the home page of your website. Set up an appointment schedule.

Execution: Set up a staging area outside the photography studio where families can wait their turn. Make sure there is a mirror in the room for last-minute primping.

Tip(s):

- Locate an online source to provide mats and frames for the photos.

- Take orders when you show the proofs, and have the materials shipped directly to the purchaser.

Variation(s):

- Find an online portrait company to handle family portrait photo sessions. Typically, your organization can sell certificates good for a free portrait in exchange for a donation ($10 or more), and the company sends a photographer out to snap the pictures and sell packages.

- Rent or ask a photo booth vendor to donate their services for a day. They bring props like funny hats and glasses that make these photos a fun, one-of-a-kind keepsake.

Success Story   An elementary school in Nebraska had great success with a family portrait fundraiser that only cost $10 per family, according to Janelle Lincoln:

> "The company that does our school pictures came in on a Saturday and took family portraits. They did an awesome job, and everyone had a lot of fun."

Did You Know?   The first known photo booth in the United States was in New York City in 1926. People lined up around the block to pay 25 cents for a black and white photo strip. Over a quarter of a million people used this photo booth in just the first six months.

---

1. Lincoln, n.d.

4. Painting Night

Give your supporters the chance to make their own masterpiece!

Description: Have you participated in a "paint-your-own" event? It's fun for people of all ages, and can be a fun activity for families to do together. Give your supporters a fun evening with their fees going to your cause. You can pay a professional to lead the activity, or hopefully get a local art teacher or artist to donate their services.

Estimated Cost:

Levels of Difficulty:

Obtaining Sponsors/Donations	⭐⭐
Finding a Venue	⭐⭐
Recruiting Volunteers	⭐⭐
Preparation	⭐⭐⭐
Execution	⭐⭐⭐

Special Materials/Equipment:

☐ Painting supplies including canvases, brushes, and paint

Sponsors/Donations: Contact a local artist or art teacher to see if they will donate their services to lead a group painting activity for a couple hours. They may be able to provide supplies, or you may get a craft store to donate them.

Possible Venue(s): School art room, or any meeting room or community room

Recommended Volunteers: At least one to take reservations and schedule the venue and artist, and a few to help at the event

Preparation: Promote the event on social media, through email, and on your website. Hang flyers in places parents will see them, like bulletin boards at churches, grocery stores, and coffee shops. Take reservations in advance to plan for the number of participants.

Execution: Set up the room as an art classroom, with the artist up front to lead the group. Make sure everyone has supplies to create their masterpiece.

Tip(s):

- Set up an event on Facebook to take reservations.

Variation(s): Hold your event at a franchise like Painting With a Twist or Color Me Mine to make it easy. They host fundraising events, provide all the supplies (and cleanup!), and donate a percentage to your group.

Web resource(s):

www.colormemine.com

www.paintingwithatwist.com

5. Student Art Gallery

Because parents love to show off their kid's art and brag about it!

Description: Partner with a school art department to hold a student art exhibition and auction off artwork in various media. Turn the event into a gala by serving hors d'oeuvres and beverages. Charge an entry fee to raise money for your organization, and auction off the art during the evening to make more money.

Estimated Cost:

Levels of Difficulty:

Obtaining Sponsors/Donations	★★★
Finding a Venue	★★
Recruiting Volunteers	★★
Preparation	★★★★★
Execution	★★★

Special Materials/Equipment:

☐ Easels, clotheslines, hooks, or stands may be needed to display art.

Sponsors/Donations:

• Ask several local restaurants to donate a few trays of hors d'oeuvres each.

• Contact grocery stores for beverage donations.

- Speak with an art or craft store about having pictures matted.

Possible Venue(s): A student art show is best held at the school itself, but a library, museum, or civic center would also work.

Recommended Volunteers: 5-10 well-dressed volunteers, including several people to pour beverages and walk around with trays of hors d'oeuvres. A professional auctioneer would be ideal, but a volunteer with a gift of gab would be fine.

Preparation: Work with the art teacher(s) to plan the exhibit. Promote the event on social media, and in local newspapers and magazines. Add a notice to the school website and your organization's website inviting people to attend. Print a program giving the names of each contributor and tags to place next to the pieces. Set an opening bid for each art piece.

Execution: Start the event with appetizers and beverages. Have the student artists available to meet the public and to stand next to their piece to answer questions and generate enthusiasm. Give attendees plenty of time to decide which pieces they like, and then auction them off to the highest bidder.

Tip(s):

- Have donation canisters on hand for those who wish to contribute directly instead of bidding.

Variation(s):

- Hold an exhibition and sale of student-made craft items.

6. Tie-Dye Event

Your Dad might think tie-dye is for hippies, but making your own creation is fun for everyone!

Description: Kids and adults alike will agree that this fundraiser is to "dye" for. Set up a tie-dying station, and let participants enjoy swirling dyes onto a rubber banded T-shirt, towel, canvas bag, socks, or other cloth item. Charge a fee per item.

Estimated Cost:

Levels of Difficulty:

Obtaining Sponsors/Donations	⭐⭐
Finding a Venue	⭐⭐
Recruiting Volunteers	⭐⭐
Preparation	⭐⭐
Execution	⭐⭐⭐⭐

Special Materials/Equipment:

☐ White T-shirts, towels, socks, or other cloth items to dye

☐ Rubber gloves

☐ Dye

☐ Squirt bottles

☐ Rubber bands

☐   Buckets of water

☐   Ziploc bags

Sponsors/Donations:

- Ask a craft store to donate tie-dye kits and items to dye.

Possible Venue(s): Any outdoor location, like a park pavilion or a table in the grass, is a good place to not have to worry about making a mess with this fundraiser.

Recommended Volunteers: 2+ to set up the station and help tie-dye

Preparation: Have volunteers wear tie-dye shirts to advertise at the event. Dye the shirts about a week in advance so you have time to wash and dry them beforehand. Tie-dye samples of each item to hang up on a clothesline with prices.

Execution: Supply volunteers with gloves and have them wear clothes that they would be OK getting dye on. Assist customers in tie-dying the items of their choice. Place customers finished products in Ziploc bags for them to take home, and give them washing instructions.

Tip(s):

- Dharma Trading Company offers group tie-dye kits with everything you need, including detailed online instructions.

- Have customers pay before they start tie dying, and designate one volunteer to handle the money.

Variation(s):

- Set up a T-shirt decorating station with puffy paint, permanent markers, or iron-on decorations.

Web resource(s):

www.dharmatrading.com

Auctions and Raffles

7. Boss for a Day

Because everybody wants to be a boss!

Description: Give a local company's employees the opportunity to sit in their boss's chair for a day or an afternoon by raffling off a top executive's job. Add to the hilarity of the event and up your bank by also requiring the boss to do the winner's job that day, including wearing a uniform, if appropriate. Choose a large company so the chances of raising a significant amount of money are greater.

Estimated Cost:

Levels of Difficulty:

Obtaining Sponsors/Donations	NA
Finding a Venue	★
Recruiting Volunteers	★
Preparation	★
Execution	★

Special Materials/Equipment:

☐ Roll of two-part raffle tickets

Sponsors/Donations:

- If you wish to offer a few more prizes, approach local retail stores, restaurants, and service providers (such as tanning salons or fitness gyms) for gift cards or other rewards.

Possible Venue(s): Large corporations and mid-sized companies, government agencies, schools and universities, and hospitals and medical centers work well.

Recommended Volunteers: 2-3 to sell tickets and conduct the raffle

Preparation: Identify target companies and make arrangements with the human resources department to schedule the event. Submit a brief article for the employee newsletter promoting the event with details about the cost, and where and when to purchase tickets. Prepare a short reminder email that can be sent to employees the day before the raffle.

Execution: Sell tickets in a high traffic area, such as the lobby or employee lunchroom. Personally escort the executive to his or her "new" job amid much fanfare.

Tip(s):

- Make sure the selected executive is onboard and has a schedule that will allow him or her to honor the commitment.

Variation(s):

- Pay to play Trading Spaces with a coworker. Trade office spaces for a few hours, and bring or buy decorations to re-do the look of their desk or cubicle.

8. Bingo Night

Everyone loves B-I-N-G-O!

Description: Host a community bingo party complete with prizes and refreshments.

Estimated Cost: $ $ $

Levels of Difficulty:

Obtaining Sponsors/Donations	★ ★
Finding a Venue	★ ★ ★
Recruiting Volunteers	★
Preparation	★ ★
Execution	★ ★ ★ ★ ★

Special Materials/Equipment:

☐ Bingo cards (available at party supply stores or for print from online sites)

☐ Plastic bingo chips

☐ Numbered bingo balls

☐ Bingo cage or other container from which to draw the balls

Sponsors/Donations:

• A bingo hall might be willing to supply bingo cards and other paraphernalia for your fundraiser, as long as it is not held on the same night as its own event(s).

- Ask several members of your organization to go to different sites online and print free bingo cards.

- Approach local businesses for gift cards and other small prizes that can be awarded to winners.

Possible Venue(s): Any room with long tables and chairs, including church halls, community centers, and school cafeterias is good. It is a plus if there is a raised platform on one end where the caller can hold court.

Recommended Volunteers: 3-4 to run the game and concessions

Preparation: Advertise the event in free community newspapers and on social media. Circulate flyers in parking lots and post them on free bulletin boards.

Execution: Charge a few dollars per game and give a discount for multiple card purchases.

Tip(s):

- Check discount department stores or toy stores for inexpensive bingo sets, or make your own bingo balls by writing letters and numbers on Ping-Pong balls with a permanent marker.

- Check with the state to see if you will need a gaming license to operate legally.

Variation(s):

- Host a bingo party for the employees of a local company.

- Add a 50/50 raffle to generate more profit (see #9).

9. 50/50 Raffle

This easy, time-tested standby helps organizations large and small make bank.

Description: This simple fundraiser entails selling tickets, drawing a winning ticket, and splitting the jackpot with the winner.

Estimated Cost:

Levels of Difficulty:

Obtaining Sponsors/Donations	★
Finding a Venue	★
Recruiting Volunteers	★
Preparation	★
Execution	★

Special Materials/Equipment:

☐ Roll of two-part tickets (available at office supply stores or online)

Sponsors/Donations: NA

Possible Venue(s): City fairs, church festivals, school events, or sporting events. You can easily add this on to another fundraising event.

Recommended Volunteers: 1-2 to handle tickets

Preparation: Buy the two-part tickets and set up a table from which to sell them.

Execution: When holding a 50/50 raffle as part of another event, like a city festival, turn it into a special event of its own. Have a display board showing how much money has been raised each hour. Make regular announcements encouraging more sales. Count down the time to the drawing, and issue a last call for tickets. To ramp up the excitement, require that the winning ticketholder be present to claim the jackpot. Then, make a special production of handing over the cash to the lucky winner.

Tip(s):

- Offer an incentive to purchase more than one ticket, such as selling tickets for $1 each, or three tickets for $2, or five tickets for $4. This will increase profits quickly.

- Check state gaming laws regarding raffles.

Success Story The Aztec, New Mexico Boys and Girls Club had an impressive final raffle pot of $33,700 with their 50/50 raffle. Read more at www.aztecbg-club.com/50-50-raffle.

10. Lunch with the CEO

This power lunch is a win-win!

Description: Auction off a meal with a well-liked and well-known CEO or other business leader in your community.

Estimated Cost:

Levels of Difficulty:

Obtaining Sponsors/Donations	★
Finding a Venue	★
Recruiting Volunteers	★
Preparation	★ ★
Execution	★

Special Materials/Equipment: NA

Sponsors/Donations:

- To maximize the amount of money your organization will realize, approach a local restaurateur to donate the cost of the meal or provide a gift certificate.

- Ask a professional auctioneer to donate his or her services to make the auction experience more exciting.

Possible Venue(s): Because audience interaction and participation are necessary to conduct a successful auction, it is best to hold it as part of another event that will attract a lot of people. A city or church festival, concert, art show, or sporting event is ideal. If the CEO is employed at a large company with many employees, a company event like a picnic or holiday party will also work well.

Recommended Volunteers: 2-3 to set up the lunch and run the auction

Preparation: Create signs to draw attention to the auction site. Promote the event in local media and social media. Send out personal invitations to potential big bidders.

Execution: Make an announcement to draw participants to the auction site.

Tip(s):

- Promote the lunch as an opportunity to network, build a relationship, or otherwise hobnob with a community business leader. Make it clear that it is *not* an opportunity to ask for a job or promotion.

Variation(s):

- Hold an online auction instead of a live auction.

- Auction off an opportunity to play golf with a popular or well-known CEO.

11. Parking Space Auction

Because people will literally fight — or pay — for a good parking spot!

Description: Auction off a prime parking spot in a company parking lot or parking structure to benefit your charity. Conduct either a live auction in conjunction with another company event, or hold a silent auction onsite.

Estimated Cost:

Levels of Difficulty:

Obtaining Sponsors/Donations	✪✪✪✪
Finding a Venue	✪✪✪✪✪
Recruiting Volunteers	✪✪✪✪
Preparation	✪
Execution	✪

Special Materials/Equipment: NA

Sponsors/Donations:

- Approach the CEO or other executive in companies that have their own parking lot or structure, especially those with assigned parking. Ask him or her to donate a spot for a set period of time (perhaps a month).

- If holding a live auction, ask a professional auctioneer to donate a small block of time for the event.

Possible Venue(s): Companies with their own parking facilities and a large number of employees are preferable so there will be a lot of bidders. Also, companies in downtown areas that offer only executive parking work well since regular staff members are likely to be eager to have a chance to get preferred parking for a specific period of time.

Recommended Volunteers: 2-3 to oversee the auction

Preparation: Advertise the auction in the company newsletter and by email. If holding a silent auction, scout out a central location in the building, and prepare bid sheets. Determine a minimum incremental bid (perhaps $1 or $5).

Execution: Decorate the auction venue (meeting room, cafeteria, gymnasium) with balloons or other decorations to create a festive atmosphere. Present the winning bidder with a token representing his or her prize, such as an oversized ticket for 30 days of parking.

Tip(s):

- Make sure the parking spot is in a premium location. If the budget allows, have a "Reserved for (Name)" sign made. You can find companies that offer affordable signs online.

Variation(s):

- Let the winner paint his or her parking spot to personalize it.

12. Quilt Auction

A one-of-a-kind handmade quilt is a treasure!

Description: Sell a hand-stitched quilt in an online auction or offer it as a raffle prize to raise funds. The quilt could be made by members of your own organization or by a person or group who donates it to your organization.

Estimated Cost:

Levels of Difficulty:

Obtaining Sponsors/Donations	★ ★
Finding a Venue	★
Recruiting Volunteers	★ ★ ★
Preparation	★ ★ ★ ★ ★
Execution	★

Special Materials/Equipment:

☐ Fabric

☐ Other quilting materials (needle and thread or sewing machine, etc.)

Sponsors/Donations:

- Ask craft store owners to donate fabric scraps for the quilt.

- Ask quilting clubs to create and donate a handmade quilt to your organization.

Possible Venue(s): Raffle tickets for quilts can be sold at another event (like a church or art fair) or through your organization's website. You can also sell the quilt through an online auction like on eBay or through Etsy, a website that sells specialized, handmade goods.

Recommended Volunteers: 3+ including experienced quilters to create quilted squares and assemble the quilt; 1 person to list the quilt on eBay or Etsy, then mail it to the winning bidder or seller; and, if the quilt is raffled, 1-2 volunteers to conduct the raffle

Preparation: Sign up for an online auction account, write an item description, and photograph the quilt. List the quilt with a reserve (minimum) price, or designate a "Buy It Now" price. If the quilt will be raffled, reserve a table for the event.

Execution: Mail the quilt once the auction closes. If raffled, display it at the event to encourage ticket sales.

Tip(s):

- Make a winter-themed quilt to remind people of the warmth it will provide in the cold weather and the festive decoration it will add to your home for the holidays.

Variation(s):

- Raffle or auction other handmade quilted goods, like placemats, table runners, or handbags.

13. Reverse Raffle

A raffle where the prize is not a prize!

Description: Imagine holding a raffle in which no one wants the prizes. That is the premise of the reverse raffle, where everyone automatically receives a chance to win a highly undesirable prize, such as a donkey, a buzz haircut, or a tacky house decoration. If they do not want the prize — which is likely if the prize is outlandish enough — they can "sell" their ticket back for a set price. This works best as part of an organization's meeting or other major event.

Estimated Cost:

Levels of Difficulty:

Obtaining Sponsors/Donations	★
Finding a Venue	★ ★
Recruiting Volunteers	★
Preparation	★ ★
Execution	★

Special Materials/Equipment:

☐ Roll of two-part raffle tickets

Sponsors/Donations:

- Find a host venue or organization where you can run the raffle as part of an event.

Possible Venue(s): Membership meetings, church and community events, and fundraising events for related causes work well.

Recommended Volunteers: 2-3 to come up with an undesirable item and sell tickets

Preparation: Promote on social media. Create a professional-looking sign to display at the event. Determine the ticket buy-back price (typically $1 to $10 or more, depending on the event).

Execution: Give attendees half of a two-part ticket and explain the raffle. Direct them to a nearby table where they can sell back their ticket. Just before the end of the event, give attendees one last chance to sell back their ticket to get a last surge of donations.

Tip(s):

- If you must award the gag prize because all tickets have not been sold back, allow the winner of the drawing a final chance to sell it back (or be prepared to load that donkey into the winner's SUV!)

Variation(s):

- Offer a real prize in addition to the undesirable prize and enter into a drawing those who "sell" back their gag prize tickets.

14. Stick Lottery

A lottery anyone can play!

Description: Raise funds by having people select a stick from among a bunch standing upright in a box filled with sand. Those who select the specially marked lucky sticks win prizes. Drawing a stick can cost $1 to $10 or more; just make sure that the higher the fee, the higher the prize values are.

Estimated Cost:

Levels of Difficulty:

Obtaining Sponsors/Donations	★ ★ ★
Finding a Venue	★ ★ ★
Recruiting Volunteers	★
Preparation	★
Execution	★

Special Materials/Equipment:

☐ Box filled several inches high with sand

☐ Large number of identical sticks, like popsicle sticks, meat skewers, or toothpicks

Sponsors/Donations:

- Ask a garden center to donate a few bags of sand.

- Approach a craft store for popsicle sticks, or a kitchenware store for meat skewers.

- Request gift card donations from stores and restaurants.

Possible Venue(s): Community and school fairs, and church and city festivals are great options.

Recommended Volunteers: 2-3 to setup up the sticks and box and to run the lottery

Preparation: Set the cost to draw a stick and the prize amounts. For example, 200 sticks at $5 will raise $1,000, so you might offer five $20 prizes, or donated gift cards in varying amounts. Using a marker, mark the ends of the predetermined number of winning sticks, and then mix them with the unmarked sticks. Insert them upright into the box of sand, making sure the colored ends are completely submerged.

Execution: Collect cash and make a loud announcement like "We have a winner!" when a lucky stick is selected.

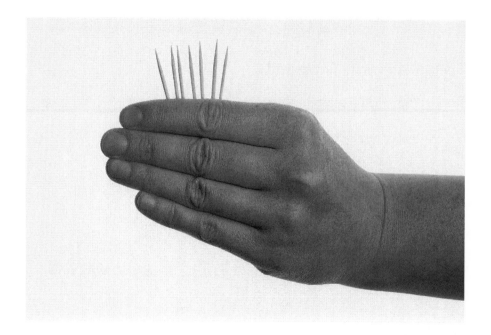

Tip(s):

- If the fundraiser is still going on when all of the winning sticks have been selected, close down the game temporarily and insert a new batch of winning sticks out of sight of the public so everyone has a fair chance to win.

Variation(s):

- Use sharpened pencils at school fairs, or golf tees at sporting events.

- Use lollipops to further entice people to participate. That way, everyone wins something.

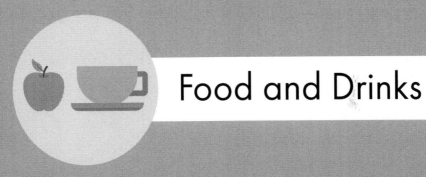

Food and Drinks

15. Bottled Water Sale

It couldn't be simpler — provide cold water to people where and when they're thirsty.

Description: The hot summer months may be the very best time for this fundraiser, but sporting events or festivals in the hot sun can be good spring or fall opportunities, too. The math is easy — buy water for 10 cents apiece and sell for $1.00.

Estimated Cost:

Levels of Difficulty:

Obtaining Sponsors/Donations	★ ★
Finding a Venue	★ ★
Recruiting Volunteers	★ ★
Preparation	★
Execution	★ ★

Special Materials/Equipment:

☐ Bottled water

☐ Coolers or tubs/buckets

☐ Ice

Sponsors/Donations:

- See if you can purchase bottled water at a discount from local grocery stores, warehouse stores, or bottled water companies.

Possible Venue(s): Anywhere there's a crowd of thirsty people, preferably out in the hot sun — think fairs, festivals, and sporting events.

Recommended Volunteers: As many as are willing to sell.

Preparation: Obtain permission from the event organizers to sell on site.

Execution: Set up a table, preferably in the shade or under a canopy, hang a sign, and sell ice-cold bottles of water from coolers or buckets; or have your members walk around pulling the cooler on a wagon.

Tip(s):

- Have members holler "Ice cold water!" or come up with an attention-getting chant.

16. Cakewalk

Because everyone loves cake, obviously.

Description: Similar to musical chairs, competitors walk around a set of marked squares and freeze when the music stops. The participants who are standing on specially marked squares when the music stops win cakes to take home. Cakewalkers pay a fee to play.

Estimated Cost:

Levels of Difficulty:

Obtaining Sponsors/Donations	✪ ✪
Finding a Venue	✪ ✪ ✪
Recruiting Volunteers	✪
Preparation	✪
Execution	✪

Special Materials/Equipment:

☐ Cakes

☐ Bakery boxes (for winners to carry cakes home in)

Sponsors/Donations:

- Call on the members of your organization to make cakes.

- Contact bakeries or grocery stores that have in-house bakery departments for donations of baked goods and cake boxes.

Possible Venue(s): Any room large enough to hold the expected number of participants, such as your organization's home, a community center, or a banquet room, works well.

Recommended Volunteers: 2-3 to bake and to run the game

Preparation: Promote the event in as many free media as possible. Prepare the cakes and make specially marked winners squares.

Execution: Tape or securely fasten the squares in a circle on the floor, creating the path participants will follow in their walk. Display the cakes, and collect participants' entry fees. Play music, stop it, and award cakes. There can be one or more winners per round.

Tip(s):

- Print a booklet containing the recipes for the cakes, and sell it for a nominal price.

- Some schools have regulations concerning homemade items. Check with your administration. If needed, you can use premade snacks like Little Debbies or bakery items.

Variation(s):

- Ask the best bakers among your donors to create more elaborate cakes, such as holiday-themed cakes or even gingerbread houses.

Did You Know? A "cakewalk" today means something that is easy to accomplish. The word originated at dances held on slave plantations in the pre-Civil War South. Slave men and women made the elaborate dance steps look easy. This practice also generated the phrase "takes the cake."[2]

2. Gandhi, 2013

17. Candy Bar Sales

It's been around so long because it works.

Description: This is an oldie-but-goodie. Don't overlook the tried-and-true candy bar sale. If you need cash quickly and your members and their families are willing to hustle for sales, this is proven to work.

Estimated Cost:

Levels of Difficulty:

Obtaining Sponsors/Donations	★
Finding a Venue	★
Recruiting Volunteers	★
Preparation	★
Execution	★

Special Materials/Equipment:

☐ Candy bars

Sponsors/Donations:

- If your members' families or your supporters can get boxes of your candy bars onto the counter at local grocery or retail stores, that will add to your sales.

- If you choose to offer prize incentives to members with the most sales, solicit a few prize donations from local businesses.

Possible Venue(s): No venue needed

Recommended Volunteers: As many as are willing to sell.

Preparation: Get as many members as possible excited about selling candy bars. Post on social media and ask members to share to generate enthusiasm.

Execution: Distribute candy bars to anyone willing to sell them, and watch the dollar bills roll in.

Tip(s):

Consider small prizes for those who make the most sales.

Variation(s):

- Offer a variety of candy beyond the standard chocolate bar!

Web resource(s):

This company, which offers no-money-up-front credit to schools, has raised more than $4 billion since 1949 with their $1 chocolate bars:

https://www.worldsfinestchocolate.com/fundraising-expertise

Household-name brand Hershey's offers their candy for fundraising, with built-in product incentives and a website full of selling tips:

https://www.hersheys.com/fundraising/en_us/home.html

18. Create a Cookbook

Home cooks love to share their recipes! Asking someone for his or her recipe is seen as a true compliment.

Description: Gather tasty recipes and compile them in a professional-looking cookbook that you can sell.

Estimated Cost:

Levels of Difficulty:

Obtaining Sponsors/Donations	★ ★ ★ ★
Finding a Venue	★
Recruiting Volunteers	★ ★ ★ ★ ★
Preparation	★ ★ ★ ★ ★
Execution	★ ★ ★ ★ ★

Special Materials/Equipment: NA

Sponsors/Donations:

- See if you can find a company that can professionally design and bind a cookbook for a discount. Several companies listed online specialize in making fundraising cookbooks at an affordable price.

- While you can solicit donations to offset the cost of compiling and printing the book, it is usually best to sell advertising pages in the book to fund the project. Local companies that recognize the value in a cookbook's long shelf life will be happy to be included.

- Additionally, you may charge each person who submits a recipe a nominal entry fee (perhaps $1 or $5) as a way to raise additional cash.

Possible Venue(s): Stores, office buildings, craft shows, or online sales through your website are good venues.

Recommended Volunteers: 10+ to collect recipes and sell cookbooks

Preparation: Collect recipes from contributors and type them into a Word document. Email the document to the company that will layout and print the cookbook. Proof the final version before printing. Also, set a retail price and draw up a distribution plan.

Execution: Bring copies of the cookbook to all organization meetings and fundraisers. Send copies to all local media that have lifestyle editors who may choose to write or talk about the cookbook. Ask local bookstores and businesses to display the book.

Tip(s):

- Arrange to sell the cookbook through Amazon.com, which handles both hard copy and on-demand books.

- Obtain advance book orders from contributors, who surely will want to see their names and culinary contributions in print.

Web resource(s):

Fundcraft Publishing has been publishing cookbooks for fundraising for more than 40 years: **www.fundcraft.com.**

This company has been publishing cookbooks for 70 years: **www.cook bookpublishers.com.**

Success Story In an article on PTO Today, Alicia Miller tells about Lawsonville Elementary, a school with 220 students, sold more than 450 cookbooks, raising more than $3,000 without any professional help.[3]

---

3. Miller, n.d.

19. Fortune Cookies

Make sure everyone gets a good fortune!

Description: Used with another fundraiser or on its own, selling fortune cookies is a fun way to generate interest in your cause. Look for a manufacturer that can produce customized messages for the cookies so you can place inspirational messages inside, along with your organization's phone number and website, and a request for a donation. Give a cookie in exchange for a donation. The cookies themselves cost as little as 10 cents each.

You can find vendors online, and you can also find recipes and instructions to make the cookies yourself.

Estimated Cost:

Levels of Difficulty:

Obtaining Sponsors/Donations	⭐⭐
Finding a Venue	⭐⭐⭐⭐⭐
Recruiting Volunteers	⭐
Preparation	⭐
Execution	⭐

Special Materials/Equipment: NA

Sponsors/Donations:

- Partner with another organization to give away cookies during its fundraising event.

Possible Venue(s): Try holding this event at community and school events and fairs.

Recommended Volunteers: 1-2 to order the cookies and hand them out for donations

Preparation: Write the custom message, place the online order, and reserve a booth or table at the community event where funds will be solicited.

Execution: Ask passersby to donate to your cause and present them with a cookie in exchange for a donation.

Tip(s):

- Time cookie giveaways or sales to coincide with the Chinese New Year (which can begin any time between late-January and early-February, depending on the year).

- Note that commercially produced fortune cookies have a shelf life of 2-3 months.

Variation(s):

- Make gourmet fortune cookies to sell through your website or online. Offer to create customized fortunes for organizations that pay extra for the service. Package them in a fortune cookie box tied with a red ribbon (red is considered lucky in Chinese culture). Check with your state to see whether you will need a food license to sell the cookies commercially.

- Make origami fortune cookies with colored paper, fill them with candy, add a paper fortune, and sell them at organization functions.

Web resource: Greenfire Products sells their highly-reviewed custom fortune cookies on **www.amazon.com.**

Did You Know? Fortune cookies are not a Chinese invention. Japanese baker Suyeichi Okamura is believed to have invented the fortune cookie in San Francisco in 1906.[4]

---

4. Yeh & Sanefuji, 2010

20. Lollipop Sale

Lollipop, lollipop, oh lolli lolli lolli...

Description: Small, portable, and inexpensive, lollipops make a great fundraising item. Typically, lollipops sell for $1 or $2 each, which is pocket change for most people, plus they come in a variety of shapes and colors. You can generate a 50 percent profit on these sweet treats, and selling them could not be easier, since everyone from kids to adults enjoys them. Add gourmet options like cherry cheesecake flavor or chocolate roses on sticks to your selection and watch the "big kids" line up.

Estimated Cost:

Levels of Difficulty:

Obtaining Sponsors/Donations	★★
Finding a Venue	★★★
Recruiting Volunteers	★
Preparation	★
Execution	★

Special Materials/Equipment:

☐ T-shirts emblazoned with your organization's logo and/or hats to identify your volunteers

Sponsors/Donations:

- Ask local businesses that cater to kids for donations. This might include pizza parlors, day care businesses, and kid-friendly hair salons. Offer to include the name of their business on your promotional materials, or affix a sticker with both the organization's and the business's name on the product.

Possible Venue(s): Schools, school cafeterias, school sporting events, dance recitals, shopping centers, malls, and community get-togethers are great.

Recommended Volunteers: 3-5+ to order the lollipops and handle sales

Preparation: Obtain permission to use a venue. Purchase the product at least two weeks in advance.

Execution: Have volunteers mingle with event participants, or set up a table near the entry to the event to attract as many potential buyers as possible

Tip(s):

- Sell hearts and/or lips lollipops around Valentine's Day.

- Sell other holiday-themed lollipops to mark occasions like Christmas, Easter, Halloween, and Thanksgiving.

- Sell sports-themed lollipops at sporting events (especially during football season).

- Add curled ribbons to the sticks to add to the presentation.

Variation(s):

- Let customers add personalized cards (provided by you) to the lollipops and offer to deliver them to the recipients in their offices or classrooms for an extra fee.

- Make your own using lollipop mix or melted chocolate, plastic molds, and sticks.

Web resource:

Famous west coast See's Candies sells lollipops to groups at at a 50 percent discount so the group can generate profits. Their website offers a step-by-step guide and a profit calculator **www.fundraising.sees.com**.

21. Popcorn Concession Stand

Who can resist the smell of freshly-popped popcorn?

Description: This popular snack comes in different flavors, offers healthy options, and can be served in sports-themed bags. It is a versatile, inexpensive fundraising food that everyone loves.

Estimated Cost: $ $ $

Levels of Difficulty:

Obtaining Sponsors/Donations	⭐ ⭐ ⭐
Finding a Venue	⭐ ⭐ ⭐
Recruiting Volunteers	⭐ ⭐ ⭐
Preparation	⭐
Execution	⭐

Special Materials/Equipment:

☐ T-shirts or hats with your organization name for volunteers to wear

☐ Money pouches and/or aprons (for holding cash)

Sponsors/Donations:

• Approach local businesses for financial assistance with product purchases. Offer to display signs at the venue to identify them as sponsors, and include their names in all other publicity efforts (news releases, ads in community newspapers).

- Request free space at venues and other places where people gather to socialize.

Possible Venue(s): Sporting facilities and playing fields, amusement parks, carnivals, shopping centers, and malls work well.

Recommended Volunteers: 3-5 to order the popcorn and run the stand

Preparation: Using the amount of money you would like to raise as a guide, order sufficient product at least two weeks before the fundraiser. Expect to pay about 50 percent of the product's retail price in your calculations.

Execution: Station volunteers at the entrance to the venue to advertise. Set up a table a few feet from the door where buyers also can stop conveniently.

Tip(s):

- Popcorn can be salty, so be sure to sell drinks and sweets to bring in more profit and complement the snack. Offer combos for discounts.

Variation(s):

- Time sales for right before the Super Bowl, World Series, Final Four, or other popular sporting events.

- Set up a retail display in a video rental store to sell packaged products.

- Rent concession equipment and pop this delicious treat right on site for hungry customers.

- Charge more for specialty bags that you dipped in chocolate or caramel or tossed in powdered cheese.

Web resource:

Many True Value hardware stores rent old-fashioned popcorn machines for as little as $40. Use the store locator to find your local store: **www. truevalue.com**.

22. Restaurant.com Gift Card Sale

Everyone's gotta eat!

Description: Your organization can order Restaurant.com gift cards for less than the value price and then sell them at the value price to make a nice profit. Customers can redeem cards online for use at 15,000 restaurants nationwide, and the cards have no expiration. You can also customize them with your organization's logo and marketing message.

Estimated Cost:

Levels of Difficulty:

Obtaining Sponsors/Donations	⭐⭐⭐
Finding a Venue	⭐
Recruiting Volunteers	⭐⭐⭐
Preparation	⭐
Execution	⭐

Special Materials/Equipment:

☐ Signs (to advertise)

☐ Table (to sell the cards)

Sponsors/Donations:

- You might ask the largest participating restaurants in your town for permission to sell cards or post a sign about the availability of the cards in their establishments.

Possible Venue(s): Retail stores, shopping centers, malls, school athletic events, community fairs, and bank and grocery store lobbies are all possibilities.

Recommended Volunteers: 3-5 to order and sell the gift cards

Preparation: Check the list of participating restaurants on Restaurant. com to make sure the gift cards can be redeemed in your area. Order the cards and promote them on your website and in your organization's newsletter. If you are selling the cards at a community event, inform the local media by sending out press releases and promote on social media.

Execution: Set up a table from which to sell the cards, with signage that a donation buys a delicious meal (or many) at any of 15,000 restaurants.

Tip(s):

- This fundraiser may not work as well in smaller towns, where there may not be as many participating restaurants.

- Around the holidays, pitch the gift cards as a perfect, low-cost stocking stuffer.

Variation(s):

- Get restaurants to donate special coupons, and sell special coupon packets.

Web resource:

http://incentives.restaurant.com/landing-pages/fundraising

Games and Contests

23. Baby Photo Competition

Name that baby!

Description: Collect baby photos from 15-20 well-known members of a social community (such as a church, school, club, or athletic association), and then take pictures of the same individuals today. Shuffle the photos and create a contest sheet showing both the old and current photos, then ask participants to match each baby picture to the current picture. Charge a fee to participate and award a cash prize. This fundraiser works best as part of another community event, such as a church fair, club activity, city fair, or anywhere else the participants are well-known.

Estimated Cost:

Levels of Difficulty:

Obtaining Sponsors/Donations	★
Finding a Venue	★
Recruiting Volunteers	★
Preparation	★ ★ ★ ★
Execution	★

Special Materials/Equipment:

☐ Digital camera (to take present-day photo)

☐ Scanner

Sponsors/Donations:

- Ask a quick print shop or office superstore to donate the printed contest sheets.

Possible Venue(s): Churches, clubs, municipal meeting rooms, schools, or membership organizations are good options.

Recommended Volunteers: 3-4 to collect photos, create the contest sheet, and sort through contestants' entries

Preparation: Contact prominent members of the target organization for baby photos, and scan the photos so they can be returned safely to donors.

Execution: During the designated community event, display the photos, charge a small fee to participate in the contest, and collect completed entry forms. Draw entries at random until you find one with a perfect score. If no one matches every picture correctly, award the prize to the entry with the most correct matches.

Tip(s):

- If possible, post the photos (or scanned copies) in a centrally located place in the organization's facility (mount them on poster board or place them under glass in a display case).

- Print the contest sheets using a high quality printer or photocopier so the picture quality is as good as possible.

24. Cutest Pet Contest

Because everyone thinks their pet is the cutest!

Description: Hold a contest to choose the cutest pet from among submitted photos. Charge a small entry fee for each contestant, and have people vote for their favorites by placing dollars into collection canisters. The person whose picture collects the most vote money is crowned "Cutest Pet" and wins a trophy or grand prize.

Estimated Cost:

Levels of Difficulty:

Obtaining Sponsors/Donations	⭐⭐⭐
Finding a Venue	⭐⭐
Recruiting Volunteers	⭐
Preparation	⭐⭐⭐⭐⭐
Execution	⭐

Special Materials/Equipment:

☐ Collection canisters

☐ T-shirts with the name of your organization (for volunteers)

☐ Signs (to promote the contest)

Sponsors/Donations:

- Contact pet stores for donations of items for the grand prize.

- Approach a sign company about donating signs.

Possible Venue(s): Pet stores, schools, or community centers work well.

Recommended Volunteers: 10+ to scan and print photos, post them, monitor donation canisters, collect and count money

Preparation: Advertise for pictures with local media, social media, and community bulletin boards. Set up a post office box to collect pictures and entry fees, or have a secure drop-off box at a central location (like a participating pet store). If displaying the photos in numerous locations, scan each photo and print the appropriate number of copies. Be sure to have one collection canister per photo. Print signs with the date of the contest and details about how to vote. At least a week before the competition, post the photos to generate excitement.

Execution: Pair up numbered canisters with a photo. Have volunteers available at each venue to explain the contest and safeguard the canisters. Award the title of "Cutest Pet" to the person whose canister has the most money.

25. Draw a Crowd

Just one sketch or caricature artist is all it takes to make this a success.

Description: You'll need to enlist services of someone who can sketch faces, like a sketch artist or caricature artist — preferably someone local who is familiar with your organization. Donors give a minimum donation to be included and email a selfie. The artist draws all the faces on a huge paper that will end up as a wall hanging or mural that can be auctioned or sold for even more money.

Estimated Cost:

Levels of Difficulty:

Obtaining Sponsors/Donations	★★★★
Finding a Venue	★
Recruiting Volunteers	★★★★
Preparation	★
Execution	★

Special Materials/Equipment:

☐ Huge paper, canvas, or the artist's preferred medium

Sponsors/Donations:

- Publicize the event continuously on social media, and tag each donor as they give.

Possible Venue(s): This can be run virtually. The only need for a venue would be a place to display and/or photograph the finished drawing.

Recommended Volunteers: One talented artist and one social media-savvy volunteer to promote online.

Preparation: Announce the event on social media, and link to the artist's website if applicable.

Execution: Set up a donations page with Go Fund Me, PayPal, or a donate button on your website. Arrange for donors to email their selfies directly to the artist.

Tip(s): Upload hi-resolution photos of each face to a site like Flickr or SmugMug so donors can purchase them to raise even more money.

Success Story In Spring 2017, local radio host and artist Larry Whitler raised nearly $12,000 for the Marion County Literacy Council in Ocala, Florida with his "Drawing a Crowd for Literacy" campaign. The finished 47-foot mural was displayed in a local public library.[5]

---

5. Whitler, 2017

CASE STUDY: LARRY WHITLER

Ocala, Florida radio host, artist, and children's book illustrator Larry Whitler calls himself a "word geek". When he heard the Marion County Literacy Council was raising money in May 2017, he figured out a unique way to help.

The project was a collaborative one which I did with my on-air partner and friend Robin MacBlane. I did all the drawing, and Robin used her organizational skills to keep track of who sent in photos, money, and special requests from donors for their drawings. She kept track of the money until it was time to turn it in.

The idea for Drawing a Crowd for Literacy truly just came to me. I've always like the dumb joke "the only thing I can draw is flies," and I wanted to use my art skills in some way to help the Literacy Council. So, after a little thought, Drawing a Crowd came to mind. I was amazed how quickly it caught on and how so many people sent in or brought in donations.

26. Dunk Tank

Every school has a principal, teacher, or coach that everyone wants to dunk!

Description: Simple to run and a lot of fun, a dunk tank fundraiser is a crowd pleaser that gives people a chance to lob balls at a target that, when hit, drops the person in the booth into the water. This could be a stand-alone event, but often works best as part of another outdoor event, such as a carnival or church fair.

Estimated Cost:

Levels of Difficulty:

Obtaining Sponsors/Donations	★ ★
Finding a Venue	★ ★ ★
Recruiting Volunteers	★ ★ ★
Preparation	★
Execution	★

Special Materials/Equipment:

☐ Dunk tank — can be rented from an inflatables company that rents bouncy houses, etc.

Sponsors/Donations:

• Solicit companies with a water tie-in (car washes, auto detailers, marinas) for donations or sponsorships.

Possible Venue(s): Carnivals, church fairs, school fairs, or city festivals are ideal.

Recommended Volunteers: 4-5 to collect money, take tickets, dole out balls to participants, and sit in the tank

Preparation: Rent the dunk tank and balls, promote the event, and line up volunteers willing to take a dip for a good cause. All "dunk-ees" are welcome, but also invite local celebrities, public officials, and school officials and teachers to participate.

Execution: Dunk tanks are popular fundraisers because they require so little work. The main tasks include selling tickets, collecting money, and handing out and retrieving balls.

Tip(s):

- Rent the dunk tank from a company that includes delivery, setup, and insurance in the rental fee.

Variation(s):

- Charge people to pie a teacher, coworker, public official or celebrity in the face in front of a crowd. Do this during an intermission at a sports game, show, or other event. Make a donation goal that must be met in order for them to be pied.

Success Story In June 2017, a retirement center raised more than $600 for an Alzheimer's charity by holding a "Dunk the Directors" tank at their annual picnic, with directors dressed in old-fashioned 1920s-style bathing costumes.[6]

---

6. Retirement Center Management, 2017

27. Executive Chair Chase

Because office workers have to do too much adulting.

Description: Challenge executives at a company to race through a relay or obstacle course while seated in their office chairs. This is best held in an outdoor location like a parking lot, but it can be hilarious when held right in the office through a maze of cubes and office equipment. Charge employees a few dollars to bet on their favorite executive, and give a prize to the competitor with the best time.

Estimated Cost:

Levels of Difficulty:

Obtaining Sponsors/Donations	★
Finding a Venue	★ ★ ★
Recruiting Volunteers	★
Preparation	★ ★ ★
Execution	★

Special Materials/Equipment:

☐ Canisters (to collect vote money in)

☐ Stopwatch (to record official finishing times)

Sponsors/Donations:

• Ask a local restaurant or other business to donate a gift certificate or other non-monetary prize that can be awarded to the chair champ.

Possible Venue(s): To raise the most money, select an organization with a large number of employees, like a corporation, government agency, large retail store, hospital and medical center, school or university.

Recommended Volunteers: 3-5 to prepare promotional materials and collect voting fees from employees

Preparation: Contact the human resources department of the target organization to propose holding a fundraiser. Create posters and emails advertising the event and submit a story to the company's newsletter to build excitement. Set a vote price (such as $1). Alert the local media, who undoubtedly will be delighted to see top executives in suits and ties engaging in such a lighthearted activity for a good cause.

Execution: Place canisters at the starting line for employees to cast their money into. Have each canister labeled with a competitor's name.

Tip(s):

- Write a post-event story for the company newsletter, listing the total amount raised, and thanking employees for their generosity and participation.

Variation(s):

- Make it an Office Olympics, and come up with other creative office games. Have a small award ceremony.

28. Fish for a Prize

Everyone gets a catch — no fishing stories necessary!

Description: Let participants cast a toy pole into a kiddie pool full of numbered plastic fish. Award them with prizes such as gift cards, stuffed animals, or bags of candy that correspond with the numbers on their fish. Charge per time they cast.

Estimated Cost:

Levels of Difficulty:

Obtaining Sponsors/Donations	★ ★ ★
Finding a Venue	★ ★
Recruiting Volunteers	★
Preparation	★ ★ ★
Execution	★

Special Materials/Equipment:

☐ Toy fishing set with poles and fish

☐ Kiddie pools or other pond-like displays

Sponsors/Donations:

• Ask restaurants and local stores to donate gift cards that you can give out as prizes.

• Ask toy stores to donate other fun prizes.

Possible Venue(s): Try holding this event at a carnival or in conjunction with a picnic. It could also be set up in a school cafeteria during lunchtime.

Recommended Volunteers: 2-3 to collect prizes, set up, and run the game

Preparation: Try to get prizes donated that vary in value. Consider setting up a few "fishing ponds" and charge more for participants to cast a pole into ponds with more expensive prizes. Create signs advertising the possible wins for each pond.

Execution: Recruit participants, collect entry fees, and give out prizes that correspond with their catches.

29. Game Night

Hook the adults with their classic childhood favorites like Monopoly, Scrabble, and the Game of Life!

Description: A friendly competition that pits teams or individual players against each other. Organizations can raise cash by charging individuals or teams an admission fee and/or by asking the host business to donate a percentage of its profits for the evening. To encourage participation, offer a prize to the winning team.

Estimated Cost:

Levels of Difficulty:

Obtaining Sponsors/Donations	★ ★
Finding a Venue	★ ★ ★ ★
Recruiting Volunteers	★ ★ ★
Preparation	★
Execution	★

Special Materials/Equipment:

☐ Board games

Sponsors/Donations:

• Ask a cafe or coffee shop to host the event and donate a prize.

Possible Venue(s): Try hosting this event at a café, school, or community center.

Recommended Volunteers: 4-5 including 1 to run the game and 3-4 to collect cash, judge the validity of answers, etc.

Preparation: Ask your organization's members and their families to borrow board games and promote the event on social media and email.

Execution: Collect admission fees at the door and take pictures of game players having a great time. If you are holding the event at a school or community center, consider selling concessions for extra profits.

Tip(s):

- Check to see if you need a gaming license from the state to legally hold such events.

- Ask the venue to offer reduced fair and drink prices to attract more players (and thus increase your organization's take of the profits).

Success Story   In 2015, the Zakat Foundation of America, together with the Muslim Homeschoolers of Chicago, held a successful student-organized family game night with the goal of raising funds to build a water well in a developing country. The event raised enough money to build two wells. A babysitting service and bake sale added additional revenue.[7]

---

7. Zakat Foundation, 2015

30. Rubber Ducky Race

Description: Release a flock of rubber duckies into a local waterway and see which ones float to victory. Charge $5 to $10 per duck and award cash prizes to top winners.

Estimated Cost:

Levels of Difficulty:

Obtaining Sponsors/Donations	✪ ✪ ✪ ✪ ✪
Finding a Venue	✪
Recruiting Volunteers	✪ ✪ ✪ ✪
Preparation	✪ ✪ ✪
Execution	✪ ✪ ✪ ✪ ✪

Special Materials/Equipment:

☐ Identical toy rubber ducks (at least several hundred)

☐ Waterproof markers

☐ Canoes and/or kayaks for duck chasing

☐ Bullhorn to announce the winning numbers

☐ Fishnets to retrieve runner-up ducks

Sponsors/Donations:

- Contact local businesses for donations to buy the ducks or offset the cost of renting canoes or kayaks. Seek corporate sponsorships for flocks of ducks.

- Ask your members' families to volunteer their kayaks and services to chase ducks.

Possible Venue(s): Any small body of water with a current, such as a stream or creek, works well. A waterway with bridges and stable banks along which people can stand to cheer on the ducks is ideal.

Recommended Volunteers: 5+ to set up, monitor the race, follow the ducks, and declare the winners

Preparation: Promote the event on social media. Number each duck on its sides using a waterproof marker. Sell ducks until just before the race begins. Keep a log of the purchasers' names and contact information so winners can be notified. Prepare posters showing who owns which duck(s).

Execution: Release the ducks at the starting line. Have volunteers take canoes and kayaks out to untangle the ducks that get stuck in the brush, and use a bullhorn to relay play-by-play commentary. To log the winning numbers and collect the ducks, station duck-catchers at the finish line.

Tip(s):

- Use ducks with a weighted base so they remain buoyant and stay upright. These tend to be a bit more expensive (about $2 each), but if you collect all the ducks at the end of the race, they can be used again.

Success Story   Windy City Rubber Duck Derby held in Chicago for Special Olympics, sells more than 50,000 ducks at $5.00 apiece to float down the Chicago River.[8]

---

8. Great American, 2017

31. Spelling Bee

*The 2016 National Spelling Bee winners spelled Feldenkrais and gesellschaft —
think your teachers and parents can spell that?*

Description: Host an old-fashioned spelling bee. Raise funds by charging
teams to enter — these events are often popular with newpaper and magazine staff. Offer a prize to the team still standing at the end of the bee.
Engage others in the event and raise more cash for your organization by
having them pay a small fee (like $1) to vote for the team they think will
be victorious.

Estimated Cost:

Levels of Difficulty:

Obtaining Sponsors/Donations	NA
Finding a Venue	⭐⭐⭐
Recruiting Volunteers	⭐
Preparation	⭐⭐⭐⭐⭐
Execution	⭐⭐

Special Materials/Equipment:

☐ Podium and a microphone (for the moderator)

☐ Two tables surrounding the moderator with a microphone on
each (for the teams competing)

Sponsors/Donations:

- Contact local companies for prizes like gift cards. Try to obtain enough prizes to award first-, second-, and third-place teams.

Possible Venue(s): Large businesses, such as corporations, government agencies, schools and universities, and medical facilities, or businesses that thrive on word play, like newspapers and advertising agencies, are great to ensure a large pool of players.

Recommended Volunteers: 5+ including a moderator and a team to come up with a list of words

Preparation: Search a dictionary for spelling words, noting the root of each word and an example of how it is used in a sentence. Choose words that are commonly misspelled or unusual rather than obscure terms. Sign up teams a couple of weeks before the event.

Execution: Set up a playing area, preferably on a stage or other raised area in an auditorium or meeting room. Invite observers to come cheer on the players.

Tip(s):

- Invite a local celebrity to serve as MC for the event.

Variation(s):

- Have a Geography, Math, or Science Bee instead.

32. Trivia Night

Because people love to show off their knowledge of useless facts.

Description: Offer players the opportunity to show off their knowledge of popular culture, current events, or general know-how in a fast-paced quiz competition. Charge an entry fee to compete, and award cash prizes to the winners. Hold the event at a school or community center, and sell snacks and beverages to keep players energized and happy. Or see if an established restaurant trivia night will hold an event to raise funds for your organization.

Estimated Cost:

Levels of Difficulty:

Obtaining Sponsors/Donations	★ ★
Finding a Venue	★ ★ ★
Recruiting Volunteers	★
Preparation	★
Execution	★

Special Materials/Equipment:

☐ Come up with your own quiz questions and answers — about 50 — as well as several tie-breaker or grand prize challenge questions, per table. See if an already-established trivia host will allow you to get in on their regular trivia night.

Sponsors/Donations:

- Approach a vending company for donations of packaged snacks, soft drinks, and water. Ask volunteers to donate baked goods for a bake sale.

- Seek a sponsor among local business owners to cover the cost of cash prizes, and tables, chairs, and microphone rentals.

- Ask a local celebrity or government official to serve as master of ceremonies/quiz master.

- Check buzztime.com to find local restaurants that hold trivia nights.

Possible Venue(s): Community centers, church meeting halls, school auditoriums, or gymnasiums are good options.

Recommended Volunteers: 5-6 to come up with questions, recruit participants, run the quiz show, and check answers

Preparation: Rent a microphone. Determine how individuals will compete (in teams or as individuals) and how long each game will run. Set up the appropriate number of tables and chairs. Create an answer sheet for each participant or team to use during play.

Execution: Have the MC call out questions. Designate a volunteer to check the answers before awarding a prize.

Tip(s):

- Hold a 50/50 raffle to increase profits. Set up a spectator area so friends and family can cheer on the players, and charge a small admission fee.

Variation(s):

- Host a topic-specific event, such as an "Earth Bowl" with geography questions.

- Host an electronic gaming competition using handheld games or PlayStations.

Web resource:

www.buzztime.com

33. Video Game Challenge

Yes, science says video games really do improve mental ability!

Description: Host a day-long video game tournament, focusing either on a single type of game or having several different game tournaments going on at one time. Charge an entry fee to play, and a small entrance fee to watch. Award prizes to the winners. Sell food and beverages.

Estimated Cost:

Levels of Difficulty:

Obtaining Sponsors/Donations	✪ ✪ ✪
Finding a Venue	✪ ✪ ✪
Recruiting Volunteers	✪
Preparation	✪ ✪ ✪ ✪ ✪
Execution	✪ ✪

Special Materials/Equipment:

- ☐ Video game consoles
- ☐ TV sets or video monitors
- ☐ Scoreboard (a chalkboard, whiteboard, or computer and LCD projector work for this)
- ☐ Sound equipment (microphone and speakers for game time announcements)

Sponsors/Donations:

- Contact video game retailers and department stores, or any type of business that caters to kids and young adults, including cell phone stores or bike shops.

- Approach businesses for gift cards that can be awarded as prizes.

- Ask grocery stores and restaurants to provide snacks and other food.

Possible Venue(s): A community or municipal center, school gym or auditorium, or restaurant is a good option.

Recommended Volunteers: 5-6 to handle registrations and collect cash, update the tournament scoreboard, sell refreshments

Preparation: Promote the event on social media and through news releases to local media and local, youth-oriented organizations. Distribute flyers and post them on free bulletin boards. Email everyone in your own organization to drum up players.

Execution: If more than one game will be played, group players by game. Update the scoreboard often. Periodically announce leaders' names. Circulate among the players to sell food and beverages.

Tip(s):

- If the challenge is for one game, have elimination rounds and a final championship round.

- If several games are underway, allow players to try to top the highest scores right up to the event's end time.

Holidays and Special Occasions

34. Corsage Sale

Because ladies love flowers!

Description: Sell traditional or wrist corsages made from artificial flowers as a lasting, wearable gift and a special expression of love and appreciation. There are a few occasions for which these are best suited: formal school dances, Mother's Day, or graduation. Set up a stand, and as potential customers arrive, ask men or families if they would like to buy a corsage for their date/mother/graduate.

Estimated Cost:

Levels of Difficulty:

Obtaining Sponsors/Donations	⭐⭐
Finding a Venue	⭐
Recruiting Volunteers	⭐⭐
Preparation	⭐⭐⭐
Execution	⭐⭐

Special Materials/Equipment:

☐ Artificial flowers

☐ Ribbons, elastic, floral tape, glue gun, pins

Sponsors/Donations:

- Florists or hobby/craft stores are perfect sponsors to donate supplies.

Possible Venue(s): If there is space, it may be easiest to assemble the corsages wherever your club meets or at a member's home. For prime sales locations, you may want to set up a stand at the entrance to dances, graduations, churches, or popular date and occasion spots.

Recommended Volunteers: 3+ to make and sell the corsages

Preparation: Plan for a one- to two- week production period (depending on how many corsages you sell) to assemble the corsages.

Execution: Bring a starter box of cash to make change. Set up your stand(s) and approach potential customers for sales. Appeal to the idea that the honoree can wear her corsage immediately.

Tip(s):

- Sales can be planned to correspond with Valentine's Day, Mother's Day, Easter, graduation, homecoming, or prom.

- Watch for sales at craft stores. Hobby Lobby often discounts their His & Hers brand corsages, and they always have 40 percent off coupons on their website for regularly-priced items.

Web Resources:

- **www.HobbyLobby.com**

- Seventeen's *7 Totally Unique Prom Corsages and Boutonnieres You Can DIY* has some easy instructions for cool corsages:[9] **http://www.seventeen.com/prom/prom-style/how-to/ a39917/diy-prom-boutonnieres-and-corsages/**

---

9. Newell, 2017

35. Holiday Cookie Dough Sale

Because all those holiday parties need cookies!

Description: Having prepared cookie dough on hand during the holidays makes it easy to serve fresh, delicious cookies to family and guests. Stress the time-saving, mess-free convenience of this crowd pleaser, and it will practically sell itself to prospective customers. There is no inventory to store and no upfront cost to your organization. Instead, you take orders for the cookie dough, which is shipped directly to the customer, and you keep a share of the profit.

Estimated Cost:

Levels of Difficulty:

Obtaining Sponsors/Donations	★
Finding a Venue	★ ★ ★
Recruiting Volunteers	★ ★ ★
Preparation	★
Execution	★ ★ ★ ★ ★

Special Materials/Equipment: NA

Sponsors/Donations: NA

Possible Venue(s): Grocery store and bank lobbies, shopping centers and malls, or holiday craft shows are good options.

Recommended Volunteers: Preferably everyone in your group - the more participants from your organization that take cookie dough orders, the more money you can make.

Preparation: Go online to locate a company that specializes in cookie dough fundraisers, and request fundraising brochures and order forms. Popular cookie maker Otis Spunkmeyer offers fundraising opportunities, and their website has lots of ideas for PA announcements and sales tools, a social media toolkit, and printable posters and sales forms.

Promote your sale on social media and on your website, and send out an email with a link to purchase.

Execution: Set up a table to take orders at well-attended school events, or just send your members out with sales forms to take orders from their family and friends.

Tip(s):

- Stress to prospective buyers how easy it is to bake fresh cookies during the holidays when starting with prepared cookie dough.

Web resource(s): www.otisspunkmeyer.com/fundraising

Variation(s):

- Choose a company that sells dry cookie mix if you prefer to direct sell rather than take orders. However, be aware that there is likely to be a minimum order requirement, so order conservatively so you are not stuck with excess product.

Success Story   The Syracuse, NY Westhill High School Chorus was invited to the Smoky Mountain Music Festival in Tennessee and needed to raise funds to make the trip. 71 percent of the students participated, selling an average of 15 tubs of cookie dough each. They sold almost $30,000 of cookie dough and were able to make the trip they called "the experience of a lifetime."[10]

10. Buchmann, 2015

36. Holiday Gift-Wrapping

Even Santa's helpers need some help!

Description: Help all the tired shoppers out during the gift-giving season by offering gift-wrapping for a charge — you might even get some tips!

Estimated Cost:

Levels of Difficulty:

Obtaining Sponsors/Donations	★
Finding a Venue	★
Recruiting Volunteers	★ ★
Preparation	★
Execution	★ ★ ★

Special Materials/Equipment:

☐ Wrapping paper and gift bags

☐ Scissors

☐ Tape

☐ Ribbons

☐ Gift tags

Sponsors/Donations:

- Ask stationery stores, florist shops, card stores, and discount retail stores for donations of wrapping materials.

- Ask neighbors, friends, and organization members to donate their extra wrapping paper and other materials.

Possible Venue(s): Malls, shopping centers, and department stores of all kinds are great places for this event. Bookstores are especially good venues because the gifts are small and easy to wrap, and your wrapping supplies will go much further.

Recommended Volunteers: 4-5 who can do a neat job of wrapping. It is a good idea to have an audition for volunteers since a certain amount of patience and precision is necessary to wrap gifts well.

Preparation: Promote the event with announcements on social media and flyers in the mall or store where you'll hold the event. Write an announcement that can be read over the mall's or store's broadcast system to direct shoppers to your wrapping station.

Execution: Set up the wrapping station in a highly visible place. Display the rolls of paper so shoppers can make their choice. Talk to the people who walk by, especially those who are laden with packages, to encourage them to stop.

Tip(s):

- If you have a secure area where packages can be stored, offer to hold the wrapped packages while people shop. Charge a small fee for keeping them safe.

- Find out if there is a store, like certain Barnes & Noble stores, that will supply you with everything you need, including wrapping paper, ribbon, cards, scissors, tape, table, and a donation box.[11] All you need to supply is the volunteers, which is a huge money-saver.

Variation(s):

- Offer a gift bag option or gift basket option.

- Provide an assortment of fancy bows and ornaments to be used as decorations for an extra fee.

Web Resource: www.barnesandnobleinc.com/about-bn/sponsorships-charitable-donations/

---

11. Barnes & Noble, 2016

37. Holiday Money Tree

Sometimes money can grow on trees!

Description: Challenge people to help cover an evergreen tree with paper ornaments that they purchase to benefit your cause. While the December holidays are the best time to hold this fundraiser, it is also a cute activity for other holidays, including for Valentine's Day, St. Patrick's Day, Easter, Mother's Day, Father's Day, Independence Day, Halloween, and Thanksgiving.

Estimated Cost:

Levels of Difficulty:

Obtaining Sponsors/Donations	⭐
Finding a Venue	⭐⭐⭐
Recruiting Volunteers	⭐
Preparation	⭐⭐⭐
Execution	⭐

Special Materials/Equipment:

☐ Cut evergreen tree in a stand, or a potted evergreen

☐ Seasonal ornaments

☐ Paperclips or ornament hangers

Sponsors/Donations:

- Approach a mall or shopping center to sponsor the tree.

- Other potential sponsors may include companies that sell live plants, such as nurseries, florists, or grocery stores.

Possible Venue(s): A mall, shopping center, busy community center, office building, or any other place where a lot of people congregate has potential for this event.

Recommended Volunteers: 3-4 to talk to potential donors, collect money, and hang "money" on the tree

Preparation: Promote the event on social media and your website. Print ornaments in different colors and shapes (such as wreaths, shamrocks, or hearts), and indicate prices. Set up a table with a couple of chairs at the designated venue.

Execution: Ask people who pass by your table to buy a paper ornament to hang on the tree. Have the donor write his or her name on the front of the ornament.

Tip(s):

- Do not hang real money on the tree to prevent theft.

- Group ornaments by donation amount on the tree, like putting all $1 donations at the bottom, $5 donations in the middle, and so on.

Variation(s):

- The tree can also be dedicated to and decorated with local or national sports team memorabilia for use as a "Spirit Tree."

38. Pumpkin Carving

Make it easy for participants to carve the perfect pumpkin.

Description: Participants are challenged to carve an imaginative, crazy, or outrageous pumpkin right on site and can win a prize for their best effort. This fun contest is best held around Halloween or as part of a fall harvest festival. Each participant pays an entry fee of $5 or more, and supporters can vote for their favorites by paying a small fee, like $1 per vote.

Estimated Cost:

Levels of Difficulty:

Obtaining Sponsors/Donations	✪ ✪ ✪
Finding a Venue	✪
Recruiting Volunteers	✪
Preparation	✪ ✪ ✪
Execution	✪ ✪

Special Materials/Equipment:

☐ Pumpkins

☐ Signs (to promote the event onsite)

☐ Tables (to display carved entries)

☐ One canister per pumpkin (to collect voting money in)

Sponsors/Donations:

- If held at a fall festival, request complimentary space for the carving contest.

- Tap pumpkin patches and local companies for donations of pumpkins and non-monetary prizes.

- Contact a cider mill to donate cider, doughnuts, and candied or caramel apples that can be sold by your volunteers during the competition.

Possible Venue(s): Community or church festivals, state fairs, cider mills, or public parks are great options.

Recommended Volunteers: 4-5 to prepare promotional materials, collect entry and voting fees, and handle the refreshment concession

Preparation: Advertise the competition on social media, in free community papers, and on bulletin boards. Send a news release to the media. Post signs, if permitted, at the venue in advance of the event.

Execution: Set up a table where fees can be collected. Establish a refreshment concession with cider and doughnuts. Circulate among viewers to urge them to vote for the best entries.

Tip(s):

- Create categories for entries, such as best traditional pumpkin, most creative carving, most intricate entry, and so on.

Variation(s):

- Have local celebrities judge the entries and award the grand prize. Select all other winners based on how many $1 votes their fans cast.

Success Story The American Institute of Architecture Students (AIAA) at Auburn University has been holding a pumpkin carve as its main fall fundraising event for 28 years.[12]

---

12. Munson and Curry, 2016

39. Seasonal Items Sale

Success is as easy as being in the right place at the right time.

Description: Make the seasons a little more festive by selling fun, seasonal plants and items to benefit your organization. A Valentine's Day rose sale, a spring flower sale, an Easter lily sale, or a Christmas tree or December poinsettia sale are naturals. This way you can raise funds at whichever time of year you need it the most.

Estimated Cost:

Levels of Difficulty:

Obtaining Sponsors/Donations	★ ★ ★ ★ ★
Finding a Venue	★ ★ ★
Recruiting Volunteers	★ ★
Preparation	★ ★ ★ ★ ★
Execution	★ ★ ★ ★ ★

Special Materials/Equipment:

☐ Tables (to display merchandise)

☐ Cash box with startup funds

☐ T-shirts emblazoned with your organization's logo and/or hats (to identify your volunteers)

Sponsors/Donations:

- Appeal to farmers, growers, nurseries, and even florists for fresh products and wrapping materials.

- Offer a sponsorship in exchange for a cash donation.

- Ask grocery stores for donations of snack foods and beverages to sell.

Possible Venue(s): Try parking lots or grocery store and bank lobbies for small portable items. A sale held at a school event, festival, or sporting activity could be very profitable as well.

Recommended Volunteers: 10+ to help pick up and move merchandise, transport it to the sale site, handle cash transactions, and promote the sale

Preparation: Make up signs directing customers to the venue. Promote the event in free community newspapers and on bulletin boards. Inform the media about the sale and the cause it will support.

Execution: Have a full crew of volunteers onsite to quickly serve customers. Play holiday-related music. Have volunteers dress according to the holiday theme. Sell themed snacks and beverages.

Tip(s):

- Donate leftover perishable products like flowers to hospitals and nursing homes.

Variation(s):

- Hold a holiday bake sale with goodies donated by members of your organization.

CASE STUDY: ALEXANDRA SKIDMORE, SOPHOMORE, BIRMINGHAM-SOUTHERN COLLEGE

Kiss Away Cancer

Through my sorority, Zeta Tau Alpha, I've had the opportunity to do a lot of fundraising for our national charity about breast cancer education and awareness. One of the most fun events we do every year is our "go pink for breast cancer" week in October. We set up a table in front of the cafeteria and sell pink ribbons, key chains, and pink pompoms that students and teachers can take to the "pinkout" football games.

People love the "kiss away cancer" banner that hangs behind the table. We charge $1 to leave a kiss and sign their name. In the past, ZTA would provide a few tubes of red lipstick and people actually kissed the banner. However, in recent years we've cut out cartoon lips that people can write their names on and pin to the banner wherever they want. Our chapter donates all of the proceeds to the Zeta Tau Alpha Foundation, a charity affiliated with our sorority that supports breast cancer education and awareness.

40. Ugly Sweater Contest

Everyone loves the tradition first made popular by the Griswold family in National Lampoon's Christmas Vacation *and continued with Harry Potter's gift every Christmas from Mrs. Weasley.*

Description: Ugly Sweater parties are in vogue — why not host one to raise money? Charge each participant an entry fee (perhaps $5 to $10), and $1 or more to cast a vote for the most hideous holiday garb. Award prizes to the people who are the proud owners of the top three ugliest sweaters.

Estimated Cost:

Levels of Difficulty:

Obtaining Sponsors/Donations	✪ ✪ ✪ ✪ ✪
Finding a Venue	✪ ✪ ✪ ✪
Recruiting Volunteers	✪
Preparation	✪ ✪ ✪
Execution	✪

Special Materials/Equipment:

☐ Collection canisters (in which to collect vote money)

Sponsors/Donations:

- Have gift cards and other prizes donated by local businesses and vendors. To justify a large entry fee for ugly sweater-wearers ($10 or more), make sure the prizes are valuable, such as dinner for two at a local restaurant or a luxury spa treatment.

- You also can collect cash from businesses and purchase gifts on your own.

Possible Venue(s): This is best held at a school event or workplace, where the potential for good-natured ribbing and competition is highest.

Recommended Volunteers: 4-5 including people to monitor donation canisters and announce the winners.

Preparation: Contact your school administration or the human resources department of a local company and pitch the idea. Obtain collection canisters and label them with numbers.

Execution: Have the participants meet in the lunchroom or conference room at a specified time. Assign a number to each participant that corresponds to a collection container. Ask other employees to vote for their favorite ugly sweater by dropping money into the appropriate numbered container. Have a mini ceremony to award the winner and runners-up prizes after the voting is over.

Tip(s):

- Take a digital photo of each sweater in contention, print them, and affix them to the appropriate collection canister.

Variation(s):

- Have entrants submit a photo of them wearing their sweater, and hold a virtual contest online.

Did You Know? National Lampoon's Christmas Vacation was released in 1989, and has remained popular for nearly 30 years. It was an instant hit, earning more than $71 million at the box office.

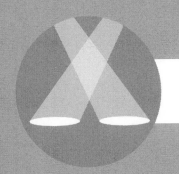

Shows

41. Dog Show

Everyone thinks their dog is the next Lassie, Benji, or Beethoven.

Description: Invite dog lovers to show off their canine pals during this fun community event. Hold either a "serious" event with qualified, professional judges or a casual event for house pets and mixed breeds. Charge a fee for each show category, offer refreshments for sale, and sell dog-related merchandise.

Estimated Cost:

Levels of Difficulty:

Obtaining Sponsors/Donations	✪ ✪ ✪
Finding a Venue	✪ ✪ ✪
Recruiting Volunteers	✪ ✪ ✪ ✪ ✪
Preparation	✪ ✪ ✪ ✪ ✪
Execution	✪ ✪ ✪ ✪ ✪

Special Materials/Equipment:

☐ Agility equipment (ramps, hurdles, barriers, etc.)

☐ Rosettes (to award to pooches who place first, second, and third in each show category)

☐ Dog bowls

☐ Plastic bags, gloves, and covered receptacles (for disposing of pet waste)

Sponsors/Donations:

- Contact pet food and toy manufacturers or pet stores for donations.

- Ask dog show judges or local breeders to donate time to judge professional events.

- For fun events, ask veterinarians or local celebrities to do the honors.

- Speak to a trophy company to acquire rosettes.

Possible Venue(s): There should be good parking and an available clean water source (to fill dog bowls) near outdoor tracks, municipal parks, or other grassy open areas.

Recommended Volunteers: 10+ to set up equipment, register entrants, judge, and run other sales

Preparation: Determine the different competition classes, which may include age, breed, or function (such as working dogs). Promote the event by sending news releases to local media and create an event on Facebook. Encourage pet owners who sign up to enter the dogs in several categories to increase profits.

Execution: Designate the main show ring. Set up agility barriers and ramps if agility events are planned. Set up and monitor dog water stations.

Tip(s):

- Beside pedigree categories, have a variety of fun categories, like prettiest dog, funniest bark, or most soulful eyes.

Variation(s):

- Make it a charity cat show or open it up to all animals, and see what interesting critters you get.

42. Family Movie Night

Give your members, their parents, and their siblings a special silver screening.

Description: Show a family-friendly film, and sell movie snacks like popcorn, soft drinks, boxed candy, and hot dogs. Hold a 50/50 raffle to raise more money.

Estimated Cost:

Levels of Difficulty:

Obtaining Sponsors/Donations	★
Finding a Venue	★
Recruiting Volunteers	★
Preparation	★
Execution	★

Special Materials/Equipment:

☐ Age-appropriate film (Rated G or PG)

Sponsors/Donations:

- Contact a local movie theater or drive-in to arrange the showing. Ask for a percentage of the ticket sales for your organization in exchange for bringing in patrons. Any other facility that has a multi-purpose room with seating and a large screen, including community centers and schools, can be considered.

- Approach restaurants, membership warehouses, party stores, grocery stores, and other businesses for donations of snack food.

- Ask a store to donate a DVD and a sign company to donate a sign announcing the event.

Possible Venue(s): Consider a movie theater, drive-in theater, church gathering room, community center, civic center, or school gymnasium.

Recommended Volunteers: 5-10 to take tickets, act as ushers, work the concession stand, and clean up after the event

Preparation: Promote the event on social media. Distribute promotional flyers throughout the community, and post them on bulletin boards. Place a sign outside the host facility at least a week in advance. Test the equipment and DVD in advance to make sure there are no glitches.

Execution: Arrange the seats in rows, pop some popcorn, open the doors, and collect the ticket money.

Tip(s):

- Check your state's copyright laws to see whether a special license is needed to show a film for profit, or show the film for free and charge for food, soft drinks, and games for children.

43. Lip-Sync Battle

Anyone can be a celebrity when you host your own lip-sync battle.

Description: Everyone wants to be an American Idol — but unfortunately, not everyone has a knack for singing. Give every frustrated singer a chance at the spotlight by holding a lip-sync show. Let participants take center stage while simply mouthing the words to their favorite songs. Charge participants a fee for the chance to wow the audience with their enthusiastic facial expressions and dance moves, and pass the hat among the spectators to gather more donations.

Estimated Cost:

Levels of Difficulty:

Obtaining Sponsors/Donations	★★★
Finding a Venue	★★★
Recruiting Volunteers	★
Preparation	★
Execution	★

Special Materials/Equipment:

☐ Sound equipment

Sponsors/Donations:

• Seek prize(s) for the winner(s) from local businesses

Possible Venue(s): School or community auditorium

Recommended Volunteers: 3-4 to play tunes, collect cash from singers, circulate in audience with donation canisters, and act as an MC to introduce performers

Preparation: Put up "save the date" signs at the venue. Promote the event on social media, local radio stations, and free bulletin boards.

Execution: Collect the entrance fee, review the song list with each singer, and treat each singer like a rock star. Have them provide their MP3 music files before the show.

Tip(s):

- Encourage contestants to promote themselves on social media and bring their own cheering section.

Variation(s):

- Encourage contestants to come dressed as a rock star or as their favorite singer and have a costume contest in addition to the lip-sync.

- Hold a celebrity lip-sync challenge, inviting well-known community leaders. Instead of charging them to sing, sell tickets to audience members.

Success Story In 2016, United Way of Marion County, Florida, held their inaugural Lip-Sync Challenge, inviting well-known locals to compete. In their second year, 2017, they raised $10,000 for their reading pals program. Contestants have included a county commissioner, local car dealers and business executives, a magazine editor, and the community college president, with performances by police officers, firefighters, and basketball players. **www.facebook.com/uwmarioncounty/**

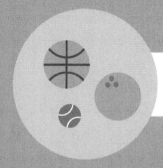

Sports

44. Bowl-A-Thon

Who doesn't like bowling shoes?

Description: Invite bowling teams, kids, families, and others for an afternoon of bowling and refreshments. This low-cost fundraiser is easy to run and requires no special equipment other than the bowling balls and rental shoes already provided at the alley.

Estimated Cost:

Levels of Difficulty:

Obtaining Sponsors/Donations	⭐ ⭐ ⭐
Finding a Venue	⭐ ⭐ ⭐
Recruiting Volunteers	⭐
Preparation	⭐
Execution	⭐ ⭐

Special Materials/Equipment: NA

Sponsors/Donations:

- Persuade your favorite bowling alley to give your organization a percentage of the money generated by supporters who attend the fundraiser.

- Contact local businesses for sponsorships in exchange for publicity at the event and in any promotional materials that are sent out.

- Ask retail businesses to donate raffle prizes and a pizzeria to donate food that can be sold to raise additional cash.

Possible Venue(s): A large bowling alley in a metropolitan area is ideal.

Recommended Volunteers: 5-10 to promote the event, collect money, run the concession, and award prizes

Preparation: Promote the event on local media, and email parents to encourage family teams.

Execution: Crank up the music, throw open the doors, and watch the money roll in. Have volunteers circulate among bowlers and offer to deliver snacks and drinks alley-side.

Tip(s):

- Find a bowling alley that offers "cosmic" or glow-in-the-dark bowling to create a party atmosphere. Consider charging a higher-than-usual flat fee to increase profits, but be sure to let participants know up front how much they must pay.

Variation(s):

- In addition to charging an admission fee, have participants collect pledges tied to their bowling prowess. Pledges can be based on the number of pins knocked down, the number of gutter balls, or some other criteria.

45. Around-the-Clock Sports Competition

Run, dance, rock 'till you drop!

Description: Challenge other groups and organizations to compete in friendly games against the members of your organization for 24 hours straight. The games could include traditional team sports like softball or playground favorites like dodgeball. Advertise to attract opponents who are well-known or beloved in the community, such as a group of firefighters or a team of the coaches from all the local sports teams. Charge each group an entry fee, and sell refreshments to spectators.

Estimated Cost: $ $ $

Levels of Difficulty:

Obtaining Sponsors/Donations	⭐⭐
Finding a Venue	⭐⭐⭐
Recruiting Volunteers	⭐⭐
Preparation	⭐⭐
Execution	⭐⭐⭐

Special Materials/Equipment:

☐ Appropriate sports equipment

Sponsors/Donations:

- Sporting goods stores, sports drink companies, and athletic apparel companies might be interested in sponsorships.

Possible Venue(s): Sports arenas or stadiums, college campuses, or shopping centers are great options.

Recommended Volunteers: 20+ since the games will run around the clock

Preparation: Include a link to an official entry form on the organization's website. Invite potential competitors personally. Advertise the event on social media and by posting notices on free bulletin boards.

Execution: Start the action at the appointed time and keep the coffee brewing and the music playing during the wee hours. It does not matter if the players are any good — just have fun!

Tip(s):

- Ask the community access cable station to cover the event or have a student videographer record so you will have footage to show to promote future events.

- Invite local celebrities like TV anchors to MC the event to generate more interest.

- Have donation boxes for each team, and encourage spectators to vote for their favorite with their dollars.

Variation(s):

- Have a 24-hour dance party or yoga-thon, and award prizes to the last ones standing at the end of the full day.

46. Earth-Friendly Fun Walk or Ride

It's healthy for participants, Mother Earth, and your group's bank account.

Description: Raise funds for your organization with a "green" fun walk or bicycle ride that promotes environmentally-friendly modes of transportation.

Estimated Cost:

Levels of Difficulty:

Obtaining Sponsors/Donations	★ ★ ★
Finding a Venue	★ ★ ★ ★ ★
Recruiting Volunteers	★ ★
Preparation	★ ★ ★ ★ ★
Execution	★ ★

Special Materials/Equipment: NA

Sponsors/Donations: Solicit sponsors among local business owners to cover the cost of the event, including snacks and T-shirts. Have participants collect pledges based on the number of miles or laps they will cover. Provide them with a simple computer-generated form on which pledges can record (see sample form and rules in the Appendices).

Possible Venue(s): Your school's track, city park, walking trail, or fairgrounds have potential.

Recommended Volunteers: 6-10 including 1 to lead the event and 5-10 to pass out T-shirts, cheer participants on, and run concession stands

Preparation: Contact a sign company to obtain a donated event sign. Establish the starting time and publicize your event in all advertising materials. Map out a safe route. Set up a (donated) tent or canopy from which to sell snacks and bottled water.

Execution: Have a ceremonial kick-off during which someone says a few words about caring for Earth and the importance of environmentally-friendly transportation. Have a cheering section to greet those who cross the finish line.

Tip(s):

- Time the event to coincide with Earth Day, which falls on April 22, or even Mother's Day as a way to show Mother Earth some love.

Variation(s):

- Combine the walk with a cleanup of a local park or roadway, and offer a prize to the team that collects the most garbage.

47. Roller Race

Invite participants to show off their boarding, blading, or scooter skills.

Description: Hold a race for participants on skateboards, roller skates, or Razor scooters. Collect an entry fee from each participant. Offer a prize to the winner. This can be a standalone event or part of a city fair or church fundraiser.

Estimated Cost:

Levels of Difficulty:

Obtaining Sponsors/Donations	★
Finding a Venue	★ ★ ★ ★
Recruiting Volunteers	★ ★ ★
Preparation	★
Execution	★

Special Materials/Equipment: NA

Sponsors/Donations:

- Contact local businesses to serve as event or team sponsors.

Possible Venue(s): Try holding this in your school's parking lot, a skate park, or city park.

Recommended Volunteers: 5-6 to set up, register participants, judge, and award prizes

Preparation: Create different competition categories such as kids, teens, or parents. Obtain permission from the city to hold the event in a city park, if applicable. Create an event on social media, and publicize with flyers at your school. If holding the event at a city park, ask the city to publicize as well.

Execution: Little work needed, other than to collect entry fees, help line up entrants, and — if it is a race — drop the checkered flag. A brief ceremony should be held to award prizes and allow pictures to be taken.

Tip(s):

- Give awards or prizes to entrants with the best themed costume.

- Sell refreshments and baked goods along the sidelines.

Variation(s):

- Pick a theme of attire for participants, like the '80s, for even more fun.

- Have a team category and allow participants to register with their group and take group pictures.

48. Halftime Contest

Get people up out of the stands for a good cause!

Description: Sell tickets for a chance to play a sports-themed game of skill during halftime at a sporting event: professional, university/college, amateur, or high school. Games can include kicking a field goal, sinking a basket, or shooting a puck. For something different, consider a potato sack race or an obstacle course.

Estimated Cost:

Levels of Difficulty:

Obtaining Sponsors/Donations	★ ★ ★
Finding a Venue	★ ★ ★ ★
Recruiting Volunteers	★
Preparation	★
Execution	★

Special Materials/Equipment:

☐ Sports equipment

Sponsors/Donations:

- Set various sponsorship levels to attract both large and small sponsors. Offer to include sponsors' names on all advertising, banners, and flyers.

Possible Venue(s): Any sports venue

Recommended Volunteers: 2-3 to set up and run contest

Preparation: Determine the timing of the event (like at the start of the game or between periods), as well as where it will be held (such as midfield or on the sidelines). Create signs to display where tickets are sold.

Execution: Sell tickets near the entrance or ticket office of the facility or field for maximum visibility. Draw a winning ticket from all entries. Provide the announcer with a prepared script giving the name of the lucky player and details about what the contest entails. Award a cash or sports-themed prize to the winner.

Tip(s):

- To keep the crowd from leaving their seats during intermission and to gain maximum exposure for your organization, minimize set-up time by having all equipment as close to the sidelines as possible and have lots of volunteers help you set up quickly while someone immediately announces what will be going on.

Variation(s):

- Offer your organization's services to professional and university sports teams to assist with tasks like taking tickets, selling food, or cleaning up in exchange for a cash donation.

- Throw a party tied to an annual event like March Madness or the Super Bowl. Charge a nominal fee to attend a big-screen TV party in your organization's headquarters, a gymnasium, or a restaurant, and charge for refreshments like hot dogs and soft drinks.

49. Polar Plunge

Invite participants to get their blood pumping to support your group.

Description: An event for the brave (and perhaps the foolhardy), the Polar Plunge is a winter endurance activity. Participants slip into their swimsuits and take a dip in a frigid body of water. Dippers raise pledges based on their ability to take the plunge or other criteria, like staying in the water for a certain amount of time or submerging completely.

Estimated Cost: $

Levels of Difficulty:

Obtaining Sponsors/Donations	★
Finding a Venue	★
Recruiting Volunteers	★ ★ ★ ★
Preparation	★
Execution	★

Special Materials/Equipment: NA

Sponsors/Donations:

- Send letters to civic organizations, clubs, and other groups to line up teams. Charge each team a small fee to participate.

- Contact local restaurants for donations of food and drinks that can be sold during the event.

Possible Venue(s): Lightly iced-over lakes, channels, streams, outdoor pools, or the ocean is appropriate.

Recommended Volunteers: 5-6 to collect entry fees (if any), run concessions, and cheer on the participants

Preparation: Set up a website to collect plunge registrations and upfront donations. Create an email template that participants can customize and send to friends and family to collect donations. Create a sign-up form that can be printed and given to teams and other participants to collect pledges (see sample form and rules in the Appendices). Promote the event to the media through news releases. Invite a local celebrity to take the first plunge at the event.

Execution: Set up a refreshment stand with food and plenty of hot drinks, including hot chocolate, coffee, and tea. Designate a location close to the water for participants and spectators to gather. Have a countdown to the plunge to build excitement. Make sure photographers are ready to take photos quickly — they won't be in the water very long! Have volunteers standing by with towels and blankets.

Tip(s):

- Offer a prize to the team that collects the most money.

- Have a microwave onsite and sell hot towels, gloves, and socks.

- Have participants sign waivers to participate at their own risk.

- Station a medical/first aid team onsite in case of emergencies.

50. Putt-Putt Golf

This hole-in-one is a win-win!

Description: Test the golfing skills of adults and kids alike by asking them to putt for a hole-in-one on a portable golfing green. This is an especially popular event during the winter, when hardcore and casual golfers alike are longing for the start of the spring golfing season.

Estimated Cost:

Levels of Difficulty:

Obtaining Sponsors/Donations	⭐
Finding a Venue	⭐⭐⭐
Recruiting Volunteers	⭐
Preparation	⭐
Execution	⭐

Special Materials/Equipment:

- ☐ Portable putting green or putt return system (available at sporting goods stores or online)

- ☐ Putters

- ☐ Golf balls

Sponsors/Donations:

- Golf equipment and other sporting goods stores may be willing to donate funds in exchange for publicity at the event. Your city's parks and recreation department is another possibility.

- In addition, ask local businesses like restaurants to donate gift certificates that you can use as prizes.

Possible Venue(s): City and church festivals, carnivals, school events, and parks work well. Also contact miniature golf courses, which may be willing to donate a part of the proceeds to your organization on the designated fundraising date.

Recommended Volunteers: 2-3 to manage equipment and participants

Preparation: Contact one of the online companies that rent 18-hole portable putting greens. Some of these companies also provide charitable organizations with a fundraising website and access to PayPal for donation collection as part of the mini-golf package.

Execution: Have volunteers wear identical polo shirts, or T-shirts with the name of your organization. Set up the portable green in a centrally located area for high visibility.

Variation(s):

- Hold an 18- or 36-hole mini-golf event. Rent a mini-golf course or locate a course that will donate its "fairway." Charge admission, and sell both per-hole and scorecard sponsorships.

- Sponsor father/daughter or mother/son tournaments, and offer a trophy or other prize to the winning duo.

51. Stair Step Challenge

Thanks to fitness trackers, everyone's trying to get in as many steps as possible.

Description: A great event for those who are fit and athletic, this fundraiser entails having participants either climb many sets of stairs or repeatedly scale one set. Funds are raised by collecting pledges based on the number of stairs climbed.

Estimated Cost:

Levels of Difficulty:

Obtaining Sponsors/Donations	★ ★
Finding a Venue	★ ★ ★
Recruiting Volunteers	★
Preparation	★ ★
Execution	★

Special Materials/Equipment: NA

Sponsors/Donations:

- Ask grocery stores, warehouse stores, or water bottling companies for donations of bottled water that you can sell, as well as donations of sports drinks and energy bars.

- Athletic shoe companies may be willing to make a cash donation for publicity at the event, which could be used for signs.

Possible Venue(s): Sports arenas, stadiums, school auditoriums, theaters, or municipal parks with outdoor staircases are good choices.

Recommended Volunteers: 5+ to keep track of participants' accomplishments, collect pledges, and cheer on the steppers

Preparation: Set a price per staircase or stair based on your fundraising goals. Promote the event and your cause through ads on social media, on bulletin boards, and by sending news releases to newspapers and radio stations. Let people register by phone or email. Create a computer-generated pledge sheet and a tally sheet that can be used during the event. Prepare climbing event T-shirts to sell at the event.

Execution: Set up a concession stand near the climbing area. Station volunteers at the bottom of the stairs to track the number of stairs climbed and to cheer on the steppers. Designate other volunteers to accept pledge sheets and onsite donations.

Tip(s):

- Check the venue's liability insurance policy to make sure the steppers will be covered in case of an accident.

Variation(s):

- Make this a team event and give a prize to the team that climbs the most steps.

52. Tailgate Party

Go, team!

Description: Find the hopping spot for tailgate parties on college or pro football weekends, or host your own tailgate party before your school's game. Set up everything fans need to kick off the game — munchies, beverages, and maybe even hats, pompoms, and other team paraphernalia.

Estimated Cost: $ $ $ $ $

Levels of Difficulty:

Obtaining Sponsors/Donations	★ ★ ★
Finding a Venue	★ ★
Recruiting Volunteers	★
Preparation	★ ★ ★
Execution	★

Special Materials/Equipment:

☐ Sport utility vehicle or truck with a tailgate

☐ Barbecue grill

☐ Charcoal

☐ Lighter

☐ Coolers

☐ Tables

☐ Folding chairs

☐ Sound equipment (to broadcast the pregame show or play fight songs)

Sponsors/Donations:

- Everyone loves football season, so it should be easy to land donations and financial sponsorships from grocery stores, convenience stores, or sporting goods stores.

Possible Venue(s): A parking lot as close to the sports event as you can get is best.

Recommended Volunteers: 5-6 to set up and run sales

Preparation: Arrive early to stake out a good spot in a visible area. Start grilling early to put fans in the mood to party.

Execution: Keep the grill stoked up and the food coming, and the event will run itself.

Tip(s):

- Set up a TV and ask for donations from people without game tickets who want to watch the game.

Variation(s):

- Obtain permission to set up a tailgate party in the parking lot of a large company during lunch on the day before a big game. Charge employees for a chance to play in a friendly game of flag or touch football, and award a (donated) cash prize to the winning team.

53. Water Balloon Fight

Kids will enjoy being kids, and adults will feel like kids again!

Make a big splash for your charity by hosting a water balloon battle. It's a fun, refreshing way to raise money during the dog days of summer, and clean up is fast.

Estimated Cost:

Levels of Difficulty:

Obtaining Sponsors/Donations	⭐
Finding a Venue	⭐
Recruiting Volunteers	⭐
Preparation	⭐
Execution	⭐

Special Materials/Equipment: NA

Sponsors/Donations:

- Ask a water-related company, such as a sprinkler company, car wash, auto detailer, or bottled water company, to sponsor the event. Besides footing the bill for the water, suggest that the company provide latex balloons preprinted with its name to increase the publicity value.

Possible Venue(s): A large open area without obstacles is great, although an area with natural barriers like bushes and trees is even better so participants can hide and ambush their opponents. A nearby water source is a plus in case the balloon supply runs low.

Recommended Volunteers: 5-8+ to collect money, fill up balloons, monitor the fight, and clean up

Preparation: The day of the event, set up an assembly line of volunteers to fill balloons, tie them off, place them in a tub or other container, and transport the container to the battlefield.

Execution: Decide whether to charge by the balloon (for example, three balloons for $5) or by the team. The latter is easier to keep track of, but you will go through a lot of balloons really fast. Assign volunteers to balloon-filling duty to keep up with demand since you may need thousands of balloons to keep the combatants armed and happy.

Tip(s):

- Use a garden hose with a nozzle to fill balloons fast.

- Purchase or rent a water balloon launcher to crank up the fun.

Variation(s):

- Organize a dodgeball fundraiser using water balloons. Entice a local celebrity or public official to serve as a willing target so paying customers can lob water balloons at him or her.

54. Workplace Mini-Golf

I'll say it again — office workers have to do Too. Much. Adulting.

Description: Turn any workplace into a miniature golf course by setting up greens that snake through the office. Include ramps, water hazards, and sand traps to tee up extra excitement. Sign up pairs and award a prize to the pair with the lowest score.

Estimated Cost:

Levels of Difficulty:

Obtaining Sponsors/Donations	★★★
Finding a Venue	★★★★★
Recruiting Volunteers	★★
Preparation	★★★★★
Execution	★★★

Special Materials/Equipment:

- ☐ Putting greens

- ☐ Golf balls

- ☐ Water and sand hazards (try Slip 'N Slides and sand-filled kiddie pools)

Sponsors/Donations:

- Contact sporting goods stores for financial donations.

- Ask a city parks and recreation department to lend equipment.

- Obtain gift certificates and other prizes from local businesses.

Possible Venue(s): Make arrangements through the human resources department of businesses with many employees, including corporations, government entities, schools and universities, and medical facilities.

Recommended Volunteers: 7+ to set up the course, register participants, and monitor the games

Preparation: Visit the venue to map out a challenging 9-hole course that will not excessively disrupt business. Measure aisles to make sure the golfing props and hazards will fit comfortably. Build or borrow mini-golf props like fake rocks or palm trees. Collect greens fees in advance.

Execution: Designate a specific tee time for each pair. Station a volunteer at each "hole" to keep score.

Tip(s):

- Schedule the event to coincide with a major golfing event, like the Masters or the U.S. Open. Have participants bring their own putters.

- Charge a participation fee based on the players' positions in the company. For instance, charge $25 for upper management pairs, $15 for middle management duos, and $10 for all other twosomes.

- Make sure the prize is significant enough to warrant the cost of the entry fee.

- Hold a 50/50 raffle to entice non-golfers to contribute to your cause.

Themed Events

55. Dress Down Day

Because kids and adults will literally pay to wear jeans.

Description: Give students or employees the option of wearing casual clothing like jeans or flip-flops outside of their normal dress code in exchange for a small cash donation (usually $1 to $5) for your organization. There are no overhead costs, so all money collected is pure profit for the organization.

Estimated Cost:

Levels of Difficulty:

Obtaining Sponsors/Donations	★
Finding a Venue	★
Recruiting Volunteers	★
Preparation	★
Execution	★

Special Materials/Equipment:

☐ Collection containers

☐ Roll of two-part tickets (to give to participants in exchange for their contribution)

Sponsors/Donations:

• It is usually easy to convince a school or business to host a casual day fundraiser since there is little work and no out-of-pocket cost involved. Talk to your school administrators or the human resources office of a company and explain why your organization needs the funds.

Possible Venue(s): Elementary, middle, or high schools, or businesses, especially those that require a uniform or have professional staff that normally wears formal business attire

Recommended Volunteers: 3-4 to advertise and collect money

Preparation: NA

Execution: On the designated casual day, send volunteers to the school or business with collection canisters. Designate a central contribution point, or have volunteers go door to door.

Tip(s):

- Give participants buttons or stickers to wear that promote your organization on the event day.

- Collect money the day before the event and give contributors a ticket as proof that they have paid.

Variation(s):

- Hold a Dress Up Day fundraiser, during which students or workers can wear as much bling and makeup as they like, or wear whatever crazy costume they wish.

- Charge a dress-down fee for employees to wear team jerseys and T-shirts on the day before a big game.

56. Kids' Sleepover

Party all night long!

Description: Host a pajama party, sometimes called a lock-in, for children at your school or another location, complete with music, games, food, and fun.

Estimated Cost:  $ if the venue is donated

Levels of Difficulty:

Obtaining Sponsors/Donations	⭐ ⭐ ⭐
Finding a Venue	⭐ ⭐ ⭐ ⭐ ⭐

Recruiting Volunteers	★ ★ ★ ★ ★
Preparation	★ ★
Execution	★ ★ ★ ★ ★

Special Materials/Equipment:

☐ Board games

☐ Karaoke

☐ Dress-up clothes (raid your closet)

☐ Age-appropriate films borrowed from the library

☐ Food (like pizza and soft drinks)

☐ Event tickets, which can be made up on a computer and printed on a copier machine to cut costs

Sponsors/Donations:

- Pizza restaurant or delivery company for food and drinks, discount stores or party supply companies for paper goods and utensils, toy stores for board games, thrift shop for unsellable clothing that can be used for dress-up.

Possible Venue(s): Consider a school auditorium, gymnasium, large classroom, church gathering center, or YMCA.

Recommended Volunteers: 1 adult for every 5-10 children at a minimum, but get as many adults who can stay overnight as possible to oversee activities and promote a safe environment

Preparation: Promote the event on social media, and send an email to parents. Create a flyer outlining what children should bring (including a sleeping bag or blanket and pillow, pajamas, stuffed animals, toothbrush, and toothpaste). Create a permission form that must be filled out, signed, and returned before the event.

Execution: Have someone tell stories and lead a sing-along. If possible, organize children by age group. Establish a firm lights-out time.

Tip(s):

- A parent or guardian who will stay overnight should accompany children who require nighttime or morning medication.

- Request details on the permission slip about allergies and relevant medical conditions, and obtain an emergency contact name and number.

- Inform parents as they drop off their children about the next morning's pick-up time.

57. Parents' Night Out

Because parents will gladly pay for a night off from the kids.

Description: Give parents a chance to enjoy a kid- and guilt-free evening out by offering babysitting services in a group setting. Offer activities for the kids like movies, arts and crafts, story-telling, and face painting. Charge a per-child fee, or set an hourly rate.

Estimated Cost:

Levels of Difficulty:

Obtaining Sponsors/Donations	★ ★
Finding a Venue	★ ★
Recruiting Volunteers	★ ★ ★ ★ ★
Preparation	★
Execution	★ ★ ★

Special Materials/Equipment:

- ☐ Arts and crafts materials
- ☐ Makeup for face painting, age-appropriate DVD
- ☐ DVD player
- ☐ Large monitor

Sponsors/Donations:

- Seek a facility with a large gathering room and bathroom facilities, and ask for permission to host the gathering, show a film, and provide refreshments like popcorn and soft drinks.

Possible Venue(s): Churches, auditoriums, school gymnasiums, or community centers work well.

Recommended Volunteers: Plan on having one babysitter for every three children who are under five years old and one adult or babysitter for every 8-10 children who are older than five.

Preparation: Make the donated room kid-friendly by removing anything with sharp edges and relocating breakable objects. Install childproof covers on accessible outlets, and clear away tripping hazards, like exposed electrical cords. Establish a firm pick-up time for parents.

Execution: Keep exterior doors locked during the event to safeguard the children. Offer one activity at a time, and conclude with a movie to reduce the activity level before pick-up time.

Tip(s):

- Create a parental consent form, and include space for medical conditions and emergency contact information.

- Ask parents to bring a blanket and pillow for kids who may zonk out before pick-up time.

Variation(s):

- Time parents'-night-out events to coincide with the holiday season to take the stress out of holiday shopping.

Sales

58. Plant a Tree

"He who plants a tree, plants a hope" — *Lucy Larcom*

Description: Instead of peddling yet another food item to your members' families and friends, offer them something unique. Planting a tree encourages families to get in touch with the earth and do something good for the environment. Consider timing your sale to coincide with Arbor Day, celebrated the fourth Sunday in April.

Estimated Cost:

Levels of Difficulty:

Obtaining Sponsors/Donations	★
Finding a Venue	★
Recruiting Volunteers	★ ★ ★
Preparation	★ ★
Execution	★ ★ ★

Special Materials/Equipment:

☐ Trees or seedlings

Sponsors/Donations:

• Speak to nurseries, tree farms, and other growers to solicit donations of tree seedlings that can be planted.

Possible Venue(s): NA

Recommended Volunteers: As many members as are willing to sell seedlings.

Preparation: Send an email to your members' families, promote on your website and social media, and hang flyers around town.

Execution: The easiest way to distribute seedlings is to give each buyer a card telling them the date, time, and place to pick up their tree. Arrange a time at your school or another convenient location and pass out the sold trees.

Tip(s):

- Distribute information pamphlets to participants that tell them how their efforts help the environment, thank them, and tell them how to donate more to your organization or get involved as a volunteer.

Variation(s):

- Sell tree and/or seed starter kits from door to door.

Web resource(s):

The Arbor Day Foundation has been encouraging people to plant, nurture and celebrate trees for more than 45 years. They offer their easy Gift Trees fundraiser:

https://shop.arborday.org/gift-trees/fundraisers.aspx

59. Baby-Clothing Sale

There's a reason children's resale shops are so popular.

Description: Kids outgrow their clothes quickly, so gently used baby clothes are always in demand. Organize a community collection effort, and resell the merchandise during a baby-clothing sale. Include shoes and accessories like socks and hats to ramp up sales, and sell refreshments like coffee and pastries to keep shoppers happy.

Estimated Cost:

Levels of Difficulty:

Obtaining Sponsors/Donations	★
Finding a Venue	★★★★
Recruiting Volunteers	★
Preparation	★★★★★
Execution	★★★

Special Materials/Equipment:

☐ Sale day signs

☐ Tables (to display merchandise)

☐ Cashbox and startup funds

☐ T-shirts (for volunteers working the event)

Sponsors/Donations:

• Ask baby clothing and department stores for donations of past-season merchandise.

Possible Venue(s): Your school, a church or community center, or parking lot in a highly visible location works well.

Recommended Volunteers: 10+ to sort clothes, organize the sale area, handle cash, and promote the event

Preparation: Advertise for donations in free community newspapers, church bulletins, and school newsletters at least a few months in advance. Store incoming donations at a designated venue. Sort and price clothing as it arrives to minimize set-up time on sale day. Create a donation receipt. Advertise the event in free community newspapers, in classified ads, and on free bulletin boards. Send a news release to the local media. Create signs with the location and day.

Execution: Place sale signs in strategic locations near the venue. Set up your table and sell, sell, sell.

Tip(s):

- Be sure to specify size availability in all advertising.

- Curtain off a corner of the venue so older kids can try on clothes in private.

- List higher-priced designer clothes or new brand-name items on eBay to maximize your earnings.

- Dispose of remaining clothing by having a bag sale (such as $10 for a full bag of merchandise) in the last hour.

Variation(s):

- Have a Back-to-School Clothes Sale of children's clothing.

60. Balloon Bouquets

"Nobody can be uncheered with a balloon."
— A A Milne

Description: Attract attention and make everyone from small kids to the young at heart happy with a colorful balloon bouquet. Balloons can be sold anywhere people congregate, but are especially appropriate at kids' parties and events.

Estimated Cost:

Levels of Difficulty:

Obtaining Sponsors/Donations	⭐
Finding a Venue	⭐ ⭐ ⭐
Recruiting Volunteers	⭐
Preparation	⭐ ⭐
Execution	⭐

Special Materials/Equipment:

- ☐ Tank of helium (purchased or rented from a party supply company)

- ☐ Balloon weights (especially for display purposes)

- ☐ Balloons (latex or Mylar)

- ☐ Colored string or ribbon

Sponsors/Donations:

- Companies that cater to children, like kid-friendly hair salons, pizza parlors, water parks, skating rinks, and toy stores.

- Craft shows might also be a good place to set up a balloon booth.

Possible Venue(s): City fairs, church festivals, or school events (i.e. sports games, dances) are great places.

Recommended Volunteers: 2-3 to fill, tie, and sell balloons

Preparation: Gather all materials.

Execution: Inflate a bouquet of balloons (10 or more) to attract interest at events or for in-store displays. Sell them on-demand and customized to each customer's preferences.

Tip(s):

- In addition to offering colored balloons, always have a varied assortment of design balloons on hand for occasions include birthdays, graduations, weddings, new babies, anniversaries, Valentine's Day, Easter, Mother's Day, Christmas, and New Year's Day.

Variation(s):

- Offer a balloon service at a hospital in concert with the in-house florist or floral provider. Deliver the balloons or bouquets directly to patients' rooms.

- Offer add-on items like candy or stuffed animals to increase the price point of each balloon sale.

61. Candle Sale

Candles are so popular they're used in seven out of 10 households.[13]

Description: Easy to organize and simple to run, a candle sale can shine a new light on fundraising for your organization.

Estimated Cost: $ $ $

Levels of Difficulty:

Obtaining Sponsors/Donations	★ ★ ★
Finding a Venue	★ ★ ★
Recruiting Volunteers	★ ★
Preparation	★ ★ ★
Execution	★ ★ ★

Special Materials/Equipment:

☐ Sample candles

☐ Tables

☐ Easel for signs

☐ Cashbox and startup funds (for making change)

---

13. National Candle Association, 2017

Sponsors/Donations:

- Contact a candle company to propose a sponsorship arrangement.

- Work with a gift store to obtain donations of past-season product.

- Ask a mall or shopping center management office to sponsor the event.

Possible Venue(s): Malls, shopping centers, grocery store lobbies, or community events like art or craft shows work well.

Recommended Volunteers: 3-4 to obtain products and sponsorships, set up the event display, sell products, and collect cash

Preparation: Advertise the event on social media, in free community newspapers, and on store bulletin boards. Send a news release to the community events editor at local papers. Price the merchandise or create signs indicating the prices.

Execution: Create an attractive display by placing small boxes or books of different sizes on the table and covering them with a tablecloth to create a landscape on which to arrange merchandise. If holding the sale in a shopping center or mall, ask the facility's management company to broadcast periodic announcements about the sale to attract buyers. Have information about your organization and business cards available.

Tip(s):

- Tie the sale in to holidays, like Thanksgiving, Christmas, Hanukkah, Valentine's Day, and Easter.

- Host a candle party with products from one of the many companies found online, which provide everything needed for a successful event.

Variation(s):

- Sell battery-powered candles.

Web resource(s): In 35 years of business, Yankee Candle Company has become one of the most popular candle companies. They've made candle fundraising easy, with online profit calculators and ordering, and will ship candles directly to your buyers:

https://www.yankeecandlefundraising.com/home.htm

62. College Care Packages

Every college student appreciates some brain food in time for finals.

Description: Offer to send care packages to college students during final exam week. Packages can include comfort food, healthy snacks, coffee, and coupons for restaurants.

Estimated Cost:

Levels of Difficulty:

Obtaining Sponsors/Donations	✪✪✪✪
Finding a Venue	✪✪
Recruiting Volunteers	✪✪✪✪✪
Preparation	✪✪✪✪✪
Execution	✪✪✪✪✪

Special Materials/Equipment:

☐ Boxes (to pack the goodies in)

☐ Return address labels from your organization

☐ Click-n-Ship labels (to mail via the U.S. Postal Service)

Sponsors/Donations:

- Contact companies that supply trial-size products to request donations.

- Talk to grocery stores or farmers' markets to purchase produce at a discount.

- Hit up the university bookstore for a monetary sponsorship in exchange for an advertising plug.

Possible Venue(s): University and college events where parents congregate are key. You can also purchase a mailing list and send a letter to solicit sales.

Recommended Volunteers: 10+ to take advance orders and pack boxes

Preparation: If selling at an event, prepare a few sample care packages that can be displayed for prospective buyers.

Execution: If the campus is a metropolitan area, hand-deliver packages to dorms or to a central drop-off point designated by the university.

Tip(s):

- Include fun stress-busters like a Frisbee or stress ball.

- Avoid sending energy drinks.

- Be sure the target university or college does not already sell a final exam package of its own.

Variation(s):

- Offer customized packages. Have purchasers fill out a simple form that requests information about students' favorites in various categories. Price the package based on the number of items selected.

- Purchase premade final exam packages from an online company; sell them at a markup to generate funds.

63. Community Rummage Sale

One man's trash is another man's treasure!

Description: Collect donated clothing, accessories, household goods, small appliances, CDs and DVDs, and other treasures, and resell them at a profit. Locate a no-cost venue and 100 percent of the profits will go to your organization.

Estimated Cost:

Levels of Difficulty:

Obtaining Sponsors/Donations	★
Finding a Venue	★★★★★
Recruiting Volunteers	★
Preparation	★★★★★
Execution	★★★

Special Materials/Equipment:

☐ Cashbox and start-up funds

☐ T-shirts with your organization's name for volunteers

☐ Tables on which to display merchandise

☐ Signs to advertise the event

Sponsors/Donations:

• The general public is the best source of donations.

- Contact retailers for donations of out-of-season or other unwanted merchandise you could sell.

Possible Venue(s): Your school, a church or community center, or a parking lot in a highly visible location.

Recommended Volunteers: 10+ to solicit donations, sort merchandise, and promote the event

Preparation: Start requesting merchandise donations at least three months in advance through ads in free community papers and the media. Designate a central collection point, such as your organization's headquarters. Create a donation receipt. Sort through merchandise as it arrives to keep the job manageable. Price individual items using preprinted tags, or place similar items in a large box at one price. Advertise the sale dates in free community newspapers and on free bulletin boards. Send a news release to the local media.

Execution: Set up your merchandise and enjoy the rush of rummagers. Have volunteers sell refreshments like coffee and doughnuts to keep shoppers energized.

Tip(s):

- Time the sale for spring-cleaning season or before the holidays, when people are looking for a last-minute charitable tax deduction.

- Donate leftover items to another organization, like the Salvation Army, to help it with its own charitable efforts.

Variation(s):

- Try setting up a trading post and charging participants an entry fee to come trade their unwanted items for someone else's treasures.

64. Custom Calendar Sale

Even with smartphone apps, most households still use a printed calendar.

Description: Proudly draw attention to your city or regional area and make money for your organization with a custom calendar sale. Select 12 outstanding photographs, work with a company to print the calendars, and sell them directly or through an online company.

Estimated Cost:

Levels of Difficulty:

Obtaining Sponsors/Donations	⭐⭐⭐
Finding a Venue	⭐⭐⭐
Recruiting Volunteers	⭐⭐
Preparation	⭐⭐⭐⭐⭐
Execution	⭐⭐⭐

Special Materials/Equipment: NA

Sponsors/Donations:

- Contact local businesses to fund the calendar in exchange for a small printed ad.

Possible Venue(s): For onsite sales, try shopping centers, malls, banks, and grocery stores. For consignment sales, approach bookstores, gift shops, and department stores. For online purchases, use an online company like Shutterfly, which creates each calendar on demand from the pictures you supply and ships them right to the purchasers.

Recommended Volunteers: 3-5 depending on whether you are selling calendars personally or using an online company to sell for you

Preparation: Identify a calendar printer and provide 12 high-quality photographs. Advertise in free shopper papers, post notices on free bulletin boards, and send news releases to radio and cable stations. Put a link to an order form on your organization's website. To encourage online sales, offer PayPal as a payment option.

Execution: Sell from a table in a frequented location, or let an online company handle sales.

Tip(s):

- Obtain photos by holding a contest for the best pictures.

Variation(s):

- Have local heroes like firefighters or sports teams pose for a calendar. This works best if you can find a photographer willing to donate his or her services.

65. Custom T-shirt Sale

This fundraiser fits everyone to a "T"!

Description: Folks are crazy for T-shirts with sports team names, sayings, and pictures, which makes T-shirts the perfect fundraising item. They may be customized to sell for specific events or created on demand and delivered later.

Estimated Cost:

Levels of Difficulty:

Obtaining Sponsors/Donations	★★★★★
Finding a Venue	★★★
Recruiting Volunteers	★★★
Preparation	★★
Execution	★★★★★

Special Materials/Equipment:

☐ Order forms

☐ Computer with internet access for taking orders

Sponsors/Donations:

• Because a customized T-shirt is a blank canvas, you can promise a potential donor space for its name and/or logo somewhere on the shirt.

Possible Venue(s): Fun runs, marathons, sporting events, or schools for custom spirit wear are great.

Recommended Volunteers: 3-5 including one who is skilled with graphic design and can create custom shirt designs

Preparation: Preprinted shirts must be designed and ordered before the event. On-demand shirts require little more than a table and a computer with internet connection. Be sure to advertise the event via news releases, flyers, and free ads in community newspapers.

Execution: There are a number of options for selling custom T-shirts. For one, you can order T-shirts appropriate for a particular event or facility, then set up a table and sell shirts to attendees. This requires an upfront financial commitment with funds recouped as you sell. Another option is to take special orders during an event, have the shirts printed, then deliver them to purchasers. This works especially well for school activities like sporting events and pep rallies. Finally, you can work with an online create-on-demand company to design a custom shirt online and personalize it while the customer waits, then have it mailed directly to the purchaser. Generally, the organization will earn a commission on that type of sale rather than a set price.

Tip(s):

- Have a sample of each size onsite so customers can try on the size shirt they want to order and make sure they will be satisfied with the fit of their T-shirts.

Variation(s):

- Sell custom sweatshirts, sweatpants, pajama pants, athletic shorts, or hats.

66. Customize a Brick

People like the chance to be part of something permanent, and especially to honor deceased loved ones.

Description: Sell laser-engraved bricks that can be installed in a prominent place, such as an entryway, walkway, patio, or wall. Because project areas tend to be large and the cost to buy a brick can be considerable, this fundraiser can raise a large amount of money for your organization.

Estimated Cost:

Levels of Difficulty:

Obtaining Sponsors/Donations	★★★★★
Finding a Venue	★★★★★
Recruiting Volunteers	★★★★★
Preparation	★★★★★
Execution	★★★★★

Special Materials/Equipment: NA

Sponsors/Donations:

- Because brick installations are practically permanent, bigger businesses may be more willing to donate to your cause. Offer them prominent positions in the installation. Also feature them in promotional materials.

Possible Venue(s): It would be great to install the bricks at your school, but any company, city building, or other venue that is building, remodeling, or updating its grounds or facility works well. Show them sample installation plans to pump up the excitement.

Recommended Volunteers: You'll need as many people to sell as many bricks as possible; 10-15+.

Preparation: Locate a company that sells and laser-engraves bricks (there are many online). Line up a venue where they will be installed. Create a promotional flyer showing how to buy bricks. Feature the promotion on your organization's website, and email information to your mailing list. Pitch the fundraiser to local media, and promote it to any publications the sponsoring venue may have.

Execution: Personally contact large donors. Sell bricks at organization and community functions. Call in to radio programs to pitch the fundraiser.

Tip(s):

- If installation of the bricks will be at a school, target parents of upcoming graduates, and advertise it as a lasting graduation gift that can be visited for years to come.

Variation(s):

- Let customers paint their own bricks instead and display them indoors for a cheaper option.

67. DVD Sale

How many times can you really watch Superman vs. Batman?

Description: Hold a drive to collect new and gently-used DVDs. Resell them to earn money.

Estimated Cost:

Levels of Difficulty:

Obtaining Sponsors/Donations	★ ★
Finding a Venue	★ ★ ★
Recruiting Volunteers	★ ★
Preparation	★ ★
Execution	★ ★ ★

Special Materials/Equipment: NA

Sponsors/Donations:

- Contact libraries and stores for donations of materials.

- Shop at used bookstores for well-priced materials you can resell.

- Send out news releases to local media informing the public that donations are being accepted.

- Ask grocery stories to donate bags.

Possible Venue(s): A school gym or cafeteria, a church basement or meeting hall, or a donated party room at a restaurant is great.

Recommended Volunteers: 10+ depending on the volume of donated materials

Preparation: Sort donated media into categories, such as action, adventure, romance, comedy, documentary, and fitness, etc. Set aside well-used materials or DVDs with cracked cases and offer them at lower prices. Make sure the cash box contains a modest amount of start-up funds (both bills and coins), so you can make change.

Execution: Set up a DVD player or laptop, and run popular movies continuously to get people in the mood to buy. If there are too many videos to display all at once, assign someone to restock the tables as the supply dwindles. Resort materials that shoppers deposit in the wrong category.

Tip(s):

- List new movies or other videos that are still shrink-wrapped in an online auction like eBay, Half.com, or Amazon.com.

- Offer unsold items at a bag price at the end of the sale, or donate them to local libraries, which can resell them during their own book sales.

Variation(s):

- Hold a pre-sale event for which shoppers pay a small entrance fee for the privilege of shopping before the general public.

68. Earplug Sale

Protecting your hearing is important!

Description: Inexpensive to buy and easy to sell, earplugs can be sold anywhere where the noise level ranges from loud to earsplitting — think concerts, air shows, and car races. Sets of earplugs packed individually can also be imprinted with your organization's name, logo, or website.

Estimated Cost:

Levels of Difficulty:

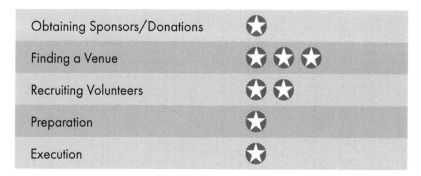

Obtaining Sponsors/Donations	★
Finding a Venue	★ ★ ★
Recruiting Volunteers	★ ★
Preparation	★
Execution	★

Special Materials/Equipment: NA

Sponsors/Donations:

- Earplugs are inexpensive — as low as 30 cents per pair. However, if you don't have funds to purchase them, solicit donations from local business owners to cover the cost.

Possible Venue(s): Any place the decibel level is high, including arena and outdoor sporting events, NASCAR and other racing events, live concerts, and air shows, is appropriate.

Recommended Volunteers: 3-4 to handle sales

Preparation: Prepare large signs for the chosen venue that feature both your organization's name and the names of your sponsors. Order the product online, and leave extra time for orders that require personalization. You can promote the event on your own social media because more attendees equals more sales.

Execution: Have a central selling point near the entrance to the event or venue. Have volunteers wear a T-shirt imprinted with your organization's name.

Tip(s):

- You can charge more for each pair of earplugs if sponsors cover the upfront cost since your organization will not have any out-of-pocket costs.

- Do not spend money on advertising since only those who attend the event will buy.

- Order ear plugs in various colors, if possible, so purchasers can select their favorite color.

69. Electronics Drive

Because no one knows what to do with their old devices.

Description: Hold a community electronics recycling drive to collect old, outdated, and broken electronic equipment, including cell phones, laptops, MP3 players, digital cameras, calculators, gaming devices, external hard drives, tablets, and e-readers. Then ship everything for free to a recycling site like YouRenew.com, which pays cash for equipment deemed to still have value.

Estimated Cost: $

Levels of Difficulty:

Obtaining Sponsors/Donations	★
Finding a Venue	★ ★ ★ ★
Recruiting Volunteers	★ ★ ★ ★ ★
Preparation	★ ★ ★ ★ ★
Execution	★ ★ ★ ★ ★

Special Materials/Equipment:

☐ Boxes (to ship the electronics to the recycler)

☐ Handcart (for moving the boxes)

Sponsors/Donations:

• Everyone has outdated and broken electronic devices collecting dust, so start by appealing to the public for donations.

- Stores that sell electronic equipment, including mobile phone stores and big box electronic stores, may also be willing to donate broken items.

Possible Venue(s): Collection sites might include a parking lot, community center, church gathering room, or your school. Ideally, the collection site should have storage space, so you do not have to move the donations more than once before they are shipped.

Recommended Volunteers: 10+ to collect, sort, and box the donated electronics for shipment

Preparation: Advertise the collection event in free community newspapers, on bulletin boards, and on your club's social media and website. Send news releases to local media.

Execution: Keep a running inventory of all donated items for your records, and immediately pack the electronics into boxes.

Tip(s):

- To gain more attention, promote the event as a green-recycling effort.

- Collect equipment on an ongoing basis to have a steady revenue stream for your organization.

Variation(s):

- Collect unfixable, unusable electronics and have people pay to enter a robot-making contest. Award prizes to winners.

70. Flower Bulb Sale

Cut flowers only last a few days. Offer bulbs so buyers can enjoy flowers for a long time to come!

Description: Late winter or early spring is the perfect time to cultivate a flower bulb fundraising effort. Your members will use colorful brochures provided by the bulb supplier to entice customers. The bulbs are shipped in bulk directly to your organization so you can distribute orders to buyers.

Estimated Cost:

Levels of Difficulty:

Obtaining Sponsors/Donations	⭐
Finding a Venue	⭐⭐⭐
Recruiting Volunteers	⭐⭐⭐
Preparation	⭐
Execution	⭐⭐⭐

Special Materials/Equipment:

☐ T-shirts with the name of organization (for volunteers)

Sponsors/Donations: NA

Possible Venue(s): Your school, community events, church fairs, or shopping centers are good options.

Recommended Volunteers: 3-5 to promote sales

Preparation: Find a bulb supplier online. Order brochures and order forms. Prepare signs to display on your table. Promote the sale on social media, in community newspapers, and hang flyers on bulletin boards.

Execution: Set up a table with signs. Place a potted plant or two on the table to put buyers in a floral frame of mind. Have volunteers greet passersby in a friendly way before hitting them up with a sales pitch. Help customers fill out order forms.

Tip(s):

- Potted plants that display the types of bulbs you are selling or a big, colorful photo attract attention.

71. Flower Sale

Who doesn't love flowers?

Description: Sell single flowers, bouquets, or potted flowers and plants as beautiful ways to brighten someone's day.

Estimated Cost:

Levels of Difficulty:

Obtaining Sponsors/Donations	✪ ✪ ✪ ✪
Finding a Venue	✪ ✪
Recruiting Volunteers	✪
Preparation	✪ ✪ ✪
Execution	✪ ✪ ✪

Special Materials/Equipment:

☐ Fresh flowers

☐ Potted flowers

☐ Plants

Sponsors/Donations:

• Ask florists, flower markets, and wholesale flower suppliers for reduced rates or free products. Because freshly cut flowers have an expiration date, florists may be willing to donate products to your organization at no cost. Be sure the flowers are not too old because you want your customers to be able to enjoy their purchase for a reasonable amount of time.

- Also ask for donations of flower food, cellophane, and ribbon for wrapping single stems. A craft store also may be willing to donate these materials.

Possible Venue(s): Anywhere people gather, including malls and shopping centers, public parks, boardwalks, tourist areas, business districts, office buildings, or your school.

Recommended Volunteers: 2-3 to obtain flowers and handle sales

Preparation: After obtaining flowers and plants from florists or flower distributors, store them in a cool place until they are used. Cut flowers should be placed in a bucket of clean water with fresh flower food.

Execution: Have volunteers wear T-shirts with the name of your organization. Set up a table or small stand in the venue of your choice. Wrap single stems in cellophane and tie with a ribbon for a pretty presentation. Tie a ribbon around flowers or plants that are in containers.

Tip(s):

- Be sure to keep cut flowers in water until they have been sold so they stay fresh.

- Time the fundraising event to coincide with a holiday like Valentine's Day or Mother's Day to increase sales.

Variation(s):

- Make artificial flower arrangements and add glitter, ribbons, and other decorations. These could be holiday-themed or personalized by writing names on the ribbons tied around the pots.

72. Fundraising Scratch Cards

The buyer gets the fun of scratching and help you make bank.

Description: You can earn a 90 percent profit with this promotion. Sell fundraising scratch cards, which have dots on them that buyers scratch off. Under the dots are various donation amounts, from zero to a few dollars. The donor chooses and scratches off a dot to uncover the amount they will pay you. Because the amounts are so low, buyers may get caught up in the fun and choose to scratch off more than one dot. If all dots are scratched off, the card totals $100.

Estimated Cost:

Levels of Difficulty:

Obtaining Sponsors/Donations	★
Finding a Venue	★
Recruiting Volunteers	★
Preparation	★
Execution	★

Special Materials/Equipment:

☐ Fundraising scratch cards (available online and can be personalized for your organization)

Sponsors/Donations:

• Scratch cards are inexpensive so many organizations simply purchase them with funds from their account. If you need to solicit sponsors for the upfront purchase, offer them the opportunity to put their name and/or company logo on the cards.

Possible Venue(s): Try this fundraiser at school events where parents will be present, set up a table outside retail stores, or sell in conjunction with other fundraising activities (such as candy bar sales).

Recommended Volunteers: Every person in the organization should be recruited to help.

Preparation: Obtain permission to set up outside a retail store.

Execution: Wear T-shirts or buttons that identify volunteers as members of your group. Have documentation available showing that your organization is a registered nonprofit.

Tip(s):

- Some scratch-card providers include a sheet of national brand name coupons that can be given to donors as a token of thanks. The donation amounts on these cards typically run from zero to $2.50 for a 60-dot card, and from $1 to $5 for a 30-dot card.

73. Magazine Subscription Drive

90percent of Americans read newspapers; you're giving them a good deal on something they already buy.

Description: Sell new or renewal subscriptions at prices greatly discounted from the retail prices. Typically, customers choose from a list of hundreds of titles, and your organization earns about 40 percent of sales.

Estimated Cost:

Levels of Difficulty:

Obtaining Sponsors/Donations	★
Finding a Venue	★ ★ ★
Recruiting Volunteers	★ ★ ★ ★
Preparation	★
Execution	★ ★ ★ ★

Special Materials/Equipment: NA

Sponsors/Donations: NA

Possible Venue(s): A venue is only needed if you decide to set up a table to sell subscriptions. This might work well on a Saturday at a busy shopping center.

Recommended Volunteers: Try to get every member in your organization to sell.

Preparation: Search online for a subscription company. Download magazine price lists and order forms. Use online tools on the subscription company's website to get social media announcements and links to online ordering.

Execution: Contact everyone you know and explain how much money they can save by subscribing or renewing magazine subscriptions during the fundraising drive. American Publishers recommends that students approach potential customers by first asking what magazines they already subscribe to, then explaining that they can renew them at a savings. That way they don't feel like they're being asked to purchase something new.[14]

Help customers fill out paperwork and collect payment, or direct them to the subscription website where they can easily order online while crediting the student. Most companies have incentive prizes for students who sell the most.

Tip(s):

- Check to see if the subscription company you have chosen will allow customers to order subscriptions on its website. Alternatively, you can choose a company that helps your organization set up a personalized website solely for selling subscriptions.

- Offer a prize to the volunteer who sells the most subscriptions to encourage friendly competition.

---

14. Beck, 2014

- An adult should always accompany children who are fundraising, especially if they are going door-to-door.

Web resource(s): One of the best-known subscription companies launched a new website in 2017 that makes it simple for buyers to purchase online. Each student is given a unique code they share with friends and family. The website also offers online toolkits for social media:

www.apmags.com

Success Story According to *PTO Today*, St. Christopher School, with only 400 students, held a magazine sale that earned them a whopping $17,000![15]

Variation(s):

- Collect like-new magazines and have a used magazine sale.

15. Beck, 2014

74. Reusable Bag Sale

Because everyone is using this greener option to plastic bags.

Description: Demonstrate your group's commitment to the environment by selling eco-friendly reusable bags. Have your logo custom-printed on the bag to advertise your cause. Depending on the supplier, your group could earn profits of 40 percent or more per bag. Because online retailers now make it easy to order online, you can avoid a big upfront cost by directing your buyers to the website to place their orders.

Estimated Cost:

Levels of Difficulty:

Obtaining Sponsors/Donations	⭐⭐⭐
Finding a Venue	⭐
Recruiting Volunteers	⭐⭐⭐
Preparation	⭐⭐⭐
Execution	⭐⭐⭐

Special Materials/Equipment:

☐ Custom-printed bags

Sponsors/Donations:

- Seek funding from grocery or retail stores that do not currently offer their own bags. Offer to include their logo on the bag in exchange for a donation.

- A recycling center might also be willing to contribute funds.

Possible Venue(s): NA if you sell online. If you choose to instead purchase bags upfront and sell them, you'd have to find a place such as outside a grocery store to sell.

Recommended Volunteers: Ask all members to participate.

Preparation: Locate a reusable bag supplier online. Some make it easy for buyers to purchase directly from their website using your fundraiser ID number.

Execution: Promote the sale on your club's social media and website, and ask all members to email friends and family and post links on their own social media.

Tip(s):

- Include a flyer about your organization with information about how to donate or help your cause in each bag.

Web resource(s):

One online retailer claims to have the biggest profit margin in the industry — 50 percent. Their site has an online ordering page for buyers, tips for success, social media tools, and success stories:

www.mixedbagdesigns.com

Success Story Parent Teacher Association members at Oak Ridge Elementary School in Lubbock, Texas were amazed at how simple and straightforward this fundraiser was for them. Their goal was $5,000, but they made $9,500.[16]

16. Mixed Bag Designs, 2016

75. Silicone Bracelet Sale

Everyone's wearing them — make sure they're wearing yours!

Description: Custom silicone bracelets are popular with the public because they declare the wearers' support for a cause and also make an eye-catching fashion statement. Come up with your own catchy slogan to put on low-cost silicone bracelet bands, or choose a custom shape or logo that represents your organization to have made into silicone rubber band bracelets (popular for trading).

Estimated Cost:

Levels of Difficulty:

Obtaining Sponsors/Donations	★
Finding a Venue	★ ★ ★
Recruiting Volunteers	★ ★
Preparation	★ ★ ★
Execution	★

Special Materials/Equipment: NA

Sponsors/Donations:

- Since silicone bracelets are quite inexpensive (often 15 cents or less each), you might be able to pay for them out of your organization's treasury. Otherwise, contact local business owners for financial support to place the order.

Possible Venue(s): Try grocery store and bank lobbies, department stores, large home improvement stores, civic center entrances, or community or church fairs.

Recommended Volunteers: 15+ including someone to order them and as many people as possible to sell the bracelets

Preparation: Prepare large signs for the chosen venue. Decide on a selling price ($1 or $2 each will usually generate the most sales). Promote the event in local media and on free bulletin boards. Sell the bracelets to your members first since wearing the bracelets will be effective advertising for them.

Execution: Have all volunteers wear a bracelet and try to sell them to everyone who approaches the building you are stationed at. Alternatively, offer them to people as they exit the building since they may feel freer to buy after they have made their primary purchases.

Tip(s):

- Order sample bracelets from several suppliers to judge the quality, thickness, width, and color before placing a full order since returns are generally not allowed.

Variation(s):

- Offer bracelets with colored letters, glitter, multi-color swirls, glow-in-the-dark, or leather options. Note that these may increase the price point of each bracelet.

Did You Know? The silicone bracelet trend may have started in 2004 when Lance Armstrong debuted yellow bracelets for his Livestrong foundation. By 2005, different colored bracelets represented awareness for different diseases: teal for ovarian cancer, red for tobacco-free kids, silver for cancer survivors, etc. In 2017, the trend is still going strong with local schools, clubs, and teams embracing the durable fashion statement, which can be purchased for as little as one cent.

CASE STUDY: TRACY CHILDERS SIMCO, FOOTBALL MOM, JACKSONVILLE, NC

With five children all active in various sports, Tracy has participated in her fair share of fundraisers. This year her fifth-grade son Caleb's community football team sold "Gray Team" silicone bracelets.

Selling the bracelets for our football team was a great success. We sold them for $2 apiece and made a profit of $400 — that will buy our tackling equipment for the season!

The kids loved buying the bracelets and wearing them to support the team. I think it helped promote team unity.

The parents actually bought the most — they loved buying them for themselves, grandparents, and other family members. Even coaches from other teams bought them to support the local football scene!

76. Special Delivery Telegrams

No, not the app. Telegrams were a real method of communication for 150 years!

Description: For the first half of the 20th century, telegrams were commonly used to send messages marking special occasions. Promote this vintage mode of communication as a keepsake; you might find a niche market with older folks that remember them. Deliver printed "telegrams" in person for events like birthday parties, graduation parties, bachelor or bachelorette parties, wedding receptions and showers, new baby arrivals, anniversary parties, retirement parties, and going-away parties. Holidays like Valentine's Day, Mother's Day, Father's Day, Grandparents' Day, and Christmas are also great times to promote telegrams.

Estimated Cost:

Levels of Difficulty:

Obtaining Sponsors/Donations	⭐
Finding a Venue	⭐
Recruiting Volunteers	⭐⭐
Preparation	⭐⭐⭐
Execution	⭐

Special Materials/Equipment:

☐ Order forms (for scheduling deliveries)

☐ Floral or balloon bouquets (offered as add-on items to increase profit potential)

Sponsors/Donations:

- You could seek monetary donations from companies whose names would appear in promotional materials in exchange for a contribution. Your organization could enjoy a 100 percent profit in return.

Possible Venue(s): Deliver telegrams to wherever the recipient is located (home, office, school).

Recommended Volunteers: 2+ depending on the number of people who pay to have a telegram delivered

Preparation: Promote a "Telegram Day" or "Telegram Weekend," so you can offer deliveries for as many types of occasions as possible. Prepare a script for each type of event.

Execution: Send out a small contingent of people from your organization to deliver each telegram. Have someone take a digital photo of the recipient getting their telegram and email it to them and the sender as a value-added feature.

Tip(s):

- Wear attire related to promoting your organization when delivering the telegram.

Variation(s):

- Offer singing telegrams. This is especially appropriate for choirs or musical groups but can be fun for anyone who has a pleasant singing voice — or the guts to belt it out in front of a group.

Did You Know? The first telegram in the United States was sent in 1844. This method of transmitting beeps representing Morse Code over wires was the first time Americans could communicate faster than a human being could carry a message.

77. Spirit Doormat Sale

We've got spirit, yes we do...

Description: Step up school spirit by selling custom doormats in your school colors. Either purchase a supply of mats to sell at school-related events or order a few samples to display, take orders onsite, and deliver mats to buyers later.

Estimated Cost:

Levels of Difficulty:

Obtaining Sponsors/Donations	★ ★ ★
Finding a Venue	★ ★ ★
Recruiting Volunteers	★ ★ ★ ★ ★
Preparation	★ ★ ★ ★ ★
Execution	★ ★ ★

Special Materials/Equipment:

☐ Signs and order forms may be needed if you are not selling online.

Sponsors/Donations:

• Since it is usually best to have the mats available for sale onsite, contact sports booster organizations, restaurants, or other businesses that sponsor sports teams, as well as stores that sell spirit gear like jerseys, to obtain enough funding to place your first order.

Possible Venue(s): School pep rallies and athletic competitions (i.e. football, wrestling, baseball, softball, volleyball, etc.) are ideal. You can even set up a table in a school cafeteria or sell the mats in the principal's office.

Recommended Volunteers: 4-5 to set up, take orders, and deliver mats

Preparation: Locate a company online that sells spirit mats. Get your school logo and verify correct team colors.

Execution: Set up a table at a school event, and sell, sell, sell!

Tip(s):

- Add a shopping cart to your organization's website, and offer the mats for sale online. Set up a PayPal or merchant account.

Variation(s):

- Sell spirit sticks, buttons, necklaces, ribbons, stickers, or temporary tattoos as well.

78. Used Book Sale

Well, not **this** *book, 'cause you're gonna want to keep it!*

Description: You can enjoy 100 percent of your profits by collecting donated, gently-used books, and reselling them to the public. Beyond bringing great reading materials to people at an affordable cost, you will also
help save trees and reduce the planet's carbon footprint by recycling.

Estimated Cost:

Levels of Difficulty:

Obtaining Sponsors/Donations	✪ ✪ ✪
Finding a Venue	✪ ✪ ✪
Recruiting Volunteers	✪ ✪ ✪
Preparation	✪ ✪ ✪ ✪ ✪
Execution	✪ ✪ ✪ ✪ ✪

Special Materials/Equipment:

- ☐ Tables to display books

- ☐ Chairs for volunteers

- ☐ Money to make change (one-dollar bills and coins)

- ☐ Locking cashbox or aprons (to safeguard money and make
  change)

Sponsors/Donations:

- Contact local libraries and literacy groups for sponsorship/ assistance. Ask libraries to donate books.

- Advertise for donations in church papers, free community newspapers, and free bulletin boards.

- Generate free publicity by promoting both donation requests and announcements for the sale on social media.

Possible Venue(s): Your school's library, cafeteria, or a community center or church meeting room would work well.

Recommended Volunteers: 5+ to collect and sell books

Preparation: Designate a collection center. Sort books by type (for example, general fiction, romance, self-help, animals, business, popular authors, and so on). Establish a price schedule, such as $1 for paperbacks and $2 for hardcovers.

Execution: Designate a table or part of the table for each category. If more books have been acquired than can be displayed at once, have volunteers restock the tables regularly.

Tip(s):

- List rare, out-of-print, or high-priced specialty books (such as art books) on Amazon.com. You must pay to list and sell this way, but you might realize higher profits by doing so.

- Put a donation jar in a conspicuous location to collect money from browsers who do not make a purchase.

Variation(s):

- Sell other media, including DVDs, CDs, or magazines.

Miscellaneous

79. Ballroom Dance Lessons

Two left feet can help you make bank!

Description: Supporters will leap at the chance to learn or brush up on their ballroom dance moves. Ask a local dance instructor to donate a week of lessons for popular dances like salsa, waltz, swing, or tango, and charge participants a fee to attend.

Estimated Cost:

Levels of Difficulty:

Obtaining Sponsors/Donations	✪ ✪ ✪
Finding a Venue	✪ ✪ ✪
Recruiting Volunteers	✪
Preparation	✪ ✪
Execution	✪

Special Materials/Equipment: NA

Sponsors/Donations:

- Find a local dance instructor who is willing to donate a week of lessons. Appeal to the idea that supporters may pay to continue lessons with the instructor, bringing in business.

- Seek a venue that will donate space for lessons for a week.

Possible Venue(s): A dance studio, gym room where fitness classes are held, or any large room with mirrors and a hard floor is best for dancing.

Recommended Volunteers: 1 to schedule lessons with the instructor and sign people up

Preparation: Find an instructor. Agree on what kind of lessons will be given, where they will take place, and when they will occur. Advertise, sign people up, and collect payments.

Execution: Have the instructor give the lessons.

Tip(s):

- Collect payment in advance. That way, you make money even if someone doesn't show up for a lesson.

- Divide groups by experience level (beginner to advanced) or by age group (children to adults).

- Think about timing: Hold this event around Valentine's Day to appeal to couples who might enjoy taking lessons together or in the spring for couples who have upcoming weddings.

Variation(s):

- Have a small performance at the conclusion of the lessons. Invite family and friends to come watch and charge an admission fee. You can also sell concessions and flowers at the show for additional fundraising.

80. Celebrity Butler

Know anyone who can pull off a real-life Downton Abbey *act?*

Description: This fundraiser depends on getting someone well known in your community to support your cause. That person is hired for gigs at an hourly rate of pay that goes to your group.

Estimated Cost:

Levels of Difficulty:

Obtaining Sponsors/Donations	⭐
Finding a Venue	⭐⭐⭐
Recruiting Volunteers	⭐⭐⭐
Preparation	⭐
Execution	⭐⭐

Special Materials/Equipment:

☐ The butler/maid/server will need an appropriate costume

Sponsors/Donations: NA

Possible Venue(s): Private parties, community events, or meetings

Recommended Volunteers: 1-2 well-known community figures, like a reporter, radio personality, or elected official

Preparation: Set up a social media account for the celebrity server(s). Promote their services, i.e. greeting guests, serving refreshments, etc., and promote them on your group's social media. Advertise their hourly rate ($25/hour is appropriate), what tasks they can do, and a contact email to hire them.

Execution: When hired for a job, the celebrity server(s) work at the party or event, telling guests about the group and project they are raising money for, and direct their employer to pay their fee directly to your group.

Tip(s):

- Have the celebrity server promote their services (and your group) on their own social media and at their job.

Variation(s):

- Enlist all your members to be servers at a well-attended community event

Success Story In Ocala, Florida, the editor of the local newspaper had the idea to be a celebrity butler to raise money for the county's literacy council. He puts on a tuxedo and posts pictures on his Facebook page of him serving refreshments at birthday parties, nonprofit events, and meetings of community organizations: **https://www.facebook.com/celebritybutler/.**

CASE STUDY: JIM ROSS, CELEBRITY BUTLER

Jim Ross, editor of the Ocala (Florida) StarBanner is on the board of the Marion County Literacy Council. He had the idea to hire himself to locals as a celebrity butler to raise funds for the organization.

I was a big fan of "Downton Abbey" and especially loved Carson, the butler. He was so droll and funny. When the literacy council needed fundraising ideas, I thought hiring myself out as a local Carson would be fun.

And I was right! People love it. They love to be served, and to pretend they are in a big manor. It's funny, but also fun. We have witty back-and-forth chats and really liven up the events. I've buttled graduation parties, birthday dinners, evening events, you name it. I charge $25 an hour, but people always pay more.

I think it's a great way to have fun, raise money for a good cause, and genuinely entertain and serve people. It's different, novel, enjoyable for all.

I joke that some day I may go from being a newspaper editor who pretends to be a butler to a butler who pretends to be a newspaper editor!

81. Cell Phone Collection

Because we all have those old phones lying around collecting dust.

Description: Collect working, non-working, and obsolete cell phones, and send them to dealers or companies that refurbish and resell them. Your charity will receive cash for each phone sent in.

Estimated Cost:

Levels of Difficulty:

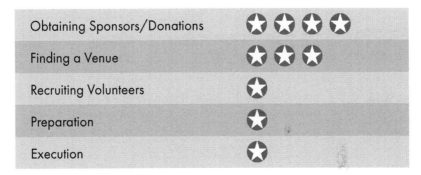

Obtaining Sponsors/Donations	★ ★ ★ ★
Finding a Venue	★ ★ ★
Recruiting Volunteers	★
Preparation	★
Execution	★

Special Materials/Equipment:

☐ Locking bins or containers where phones can be deposited securely

Sponsors/Donations:

• Ask individuals to donate cell phones.

• Contact large organizations that employ teams of salespeople, since they are likely to update their electronic equipment regularly and may be willing to donate phones to your cause.

- Ask local mobile phone stores if you could place a collection bin in their store.

- Appeal to an organization or maintenance equipment store to donate locking bins.

Possible Venue(s): Install collection bins at your school, grocery stores, bank lobbies, libraries, and electronics stores.

Recommended Volunteers: 1+ to set up a collection spot. Encourage everyone in your organization to collect phones for your organization as well as to donate their own old phones.

Preparation: Obtain and install bins in selected locations. Promote the collection dates on social media.

Execution: Set a collection deadline. Box up phones as they come in and ship them to the selected dealer.

Tip(s):

- Emphasize how recycling old phones helps the environment by keeping them out of landfills.

- Promote how the funds will be used by your organization.

Variation(s):

- Select a recycling company that accepts ink cartridges along with phones to increase your organization's profit potential.

- Partner with an entertainment venue like a movie theater or community playhouse to offer discounted admission to patrons who donate a phone.

Web resource(s): There are many companies online that pay school groups for old cell phones. One site that includes testimonials from more than a dozen groups is **www.phoneraiser.com**

Success Story The Legacy High School cheerleaders in Broomfield, Colorado, say that parents placing collection boxes at their workplaces is key to their success with this event. They say that this fundraiser pays the team's ongoing expenses and allows them to travel to the national competition.[17]

17. Phoneraiser, 2016

82. Charity Buzz Cut

Harry Styles, Justin Bieber, and Jessie J have all cut their hair for charity.

Description: Find a volunteer willing to have his or her head shaved for charity. Set a lofty monetary goal, and challenge the community to meet it. Once the goal has been met, hold an event in a public setting during which the volunteer loses his or her locks with plenty of fanfare.

Estimated Cost: $

Levels of Difficulty:

Obtaining Sponsors/Donations	★
Finding a Venue	★
Recruiting Volunteers	★ ★ ★ ★ ★
Preparation	★
Execution	★

Special Materials/Equipment:

☐ Stylist's cape

☐ Razor or sharp pair of shears

Sponsors/Donations:

• Ask a stylist who has a lot of personal flair to donate his or her services for the big snip.

- Contact a local band to provide music during the event.

Possible Venue(s): A community center, city park, city or church festival, or televised city council meeting has potential.

Recommended Volunteers: 5-10+ to solicit funds

Preparation: Find a recognizable community leader, popular sports figure, or media personality who would be willing to make a big sacrifice for charity. Promote the event heavily to local media, playing up the charitable angle and the identity of the person who will be shorn and emphasizing how to donate. Take online donations through PayPal or create a Go Fund Me page.

Execution: Make the event into a community celebration, and invite the media to attend. Sell refreshments. Make an announcement concerning the amount of money raised; then have the person who will have their head shaved make a grand entrance.

Tip(s):

- Make a final pass with a collection canister among people in attendance to garner last minute donations.

- If the person being shaved has long hair, save the shorn hair so it can be donated to an organization like Wigs for Kids, which provides wigs for children with serious medical conditions.

Variation(s):

Make it a Charity Dye, for which someone agrees to dye his or her hair an outrageous color if the fund-raising goal is met.

Did You Know? Actress Gina Rodriguez promoted her haircut and Locks of Love donation to her nearly 2 million Instagram followers in May 2016. She was later featured with her partially-shaved hairdo on the cover of *Latina* magazine.

83. Clothing Drive/Recycling Collection

Clean out your closet! Designer labels and clearance sale specials are all worth money for recycling.

Description: Did you know your unwanted clothing can be donated to go to people in Africa, keeping it out of landfills, and can earn cash for your group?

Estimated Cost:

Levels of Difficulty:

Obtaining Sponsors/Donations	⭐
Finding a Venue	⭐⭐⭐
Recruiting Volunteers	⭐⭐
Preparation	⭐⭐
Execution	⭐⭐

Special Materials/Equipment: All you need is a place to collect donations. They don't even need to be hung up.

Sponsors/Donations:

- You are looking for donations of used clothing — the more the better. The purchase value and condition of the clothes is not important.

Possible Venue(s): You may want to collect the clothing at your school; however you will need a place to stores the clothes during the collection. If you don't have room in your school building, that could be someone's garage or storage unit.

Recommended Volunteers: All your members should promote the collection. You'll need at least a few volunteers onsite during the day(s) the public is bringing in donations, and a few to weigh and ship the clothing.

Preparation: Promote your public collection day(s) on social media; create an event and send invitations on social media or via email. Hang flyers at school.

Execution: On your designated public collection day(s), make it easy for donors to pull up in their cars with their donations. Have volunteers get the clothing out of their trunk and carry it in.

Tip(s):

- When publicizing, be sure to explain that this is a win-win fundraiser: you are collecting unused clothing to raise money for your project, but the clothing will go to impoverished third-world countries to be distributed to people who need it.

Web resource(s): There are many companies online. One that has an easy-to-use website and good Facebook reviews is **www.clothingdrive fundraiser.com**.

Variation(s):

- Collect shoes instead or in addition to clothing; there are many organizations online including **https://angelbins.com**.

84. Container Collection

It couldn't be easier.

Description: This simple fundraiser has the potential to raise big money with minimal effort. Just place labeled collection containers in prominent (and protected) locations and wait for contributions to roll in.

Estimated Cost:

Levels of Difficulty:

Obtaining Sponsors/Donations	★
Finding a Venue	★
Recruiting Volunteers	★
Preparation	★
Execution	★

Special Materials/Equipment:

☐ Labeled containers (inexpensive and readily available online)

Sponsors/Donations:

- While sponsors are not necessary for this low-cost fundraiser, your organization certainly can solicit a donation from any store or facility where the collection jars are placed.

- In addition, you could ask business owners to contribute to cover the cost of the collection containers.

Possible Venue(s): Convenience stores, department stores, libraries, churches, or other service businesses like dry cleaners, pharmacies, and gas stations work well.

Recommended Volunteers: 4-5 to place and regularly retrieve collection containers

Preparation: Order fundraising containers. Apply a label with your organization' name, phone number, and fundraiser name on each container. Contact businesses to request permission to place a container on their counter for a set amount of time.

Execution: Deliver the containers to the pre-arranged locations. Periodically check to see if they contain a lot of cash, so it can be removed and deposited in your organization's account. Retrieve the containers at the end of the fundraising effort.

Tip(s):

- Always use professional fundraiser containers, which look more businesslike than homemade containers.

- Make sure they are located in a safe location, so they are accessible to donors, but are not an easy target for thieves.

- Because this is a passive fundraiser, leave the containers out for a few weeks, then rotate them to new locations periodically to increase visibility and widen the donation range.

Variation(s):

- Ask stores to ask customers if they'd like to donate a dollar and get their name written on a piece of paper in the shape of your logo or a heart, which will be displayed in the store.

85. Dollar Days

Make bank one buck at a time.

Description: These days, it may seem like a dollar does not buy much, but it can do wonders for your organization. This fundraiser encourages potential donors to contribute a dollar per day for a specified period of time, such as a week or two. Hold the fundraiser at your school and challenge parents to match their students' donations to double your organization's take.

Estimated Cost:

Levels of Difficulty:

Obtaining Sponsors/Donations	⭐⭐
Finding a Venue	⭐⭐
Recruiting Volunteers	⭐
Preparation	⭐
Execution	⭐

Special Materials/Equipment:

☐ Containers, bank bags, or cash boxes to collect money

Sponsors/Donations:

- Ask radio or TV stations to promote the fundraiser, especially during the morning drive time when working adults are tuned in, and invite listeners or watchers to call in a pledge, or visit your website to donate.

Possible Venue(s): Schools are ideal venues because of the possibility of asking parents to match their children's donations. Other venues might include businesses, medical facilities, government offices, community events, churches, and shopping centers.

Recommended Volunteers: 3-4 to make announcements and collect money

Preparation: Promote the specific dates of your fundraiser on social media and encourage your members to share. Hang flyers at school and, if possible, send an email to parents.

Execution: Unveil the fundraising idea to attendees during a regularly scheduled meeting or assembly, or at a special event. Each day of the fundraiser have your members collect donations.

Tip(s):

- Send emails to parents with the amount of their children's donations so they can match donations, and include information about the easiest way for them to contact you with payment.

Variation(s):

- Try for $5 or $10 days to generate more donations.

86. Email Campaign

Keep 100 percent of the profits — it won't cost you a cent.

Description: The simplest way to raise money is just to ask for it. Send a well-written email to everyone you can think of, explaining why you're raising money and how much you need.

Estimated Cost:

Levels of Difficulty:

Obtaining Sponsors/Donations	★
Finding a Venue	★
Recruiting Volunteers	★ ★ ★
Preparation	★
Execution	★

Special Materials/Equipment:

☐ Free bulk email program like **www.Mailchimp.com**

Sponsors/Donations: NA

Possible Venue(s): NA

Recommended Volunteers: 1 good writer to draft the text of the email, 1 design-savvy person to create the email with photos and layouts, 1 quick typist to enter the list, and all your members to contribute email addresses of potential donors.

Preparation: Ask all members of your group to compile a list of email addresses for family, friends, and local business people who might be able to donate.

Execution: Copy and paste all the email addresses into the email program. The design volunteer can craft a visually-appealing message including text explaining how much money you need to raise, and why you need it. Include a "Donate" button that links to a GoFundMe page, PayPal, or an online shopping cart, so donors can contribute immediately with their credit card.

Tip(s):

- Email programs like Gmail see large mailing lists as spam. Sign up for a free bulk mailer account like MailChimp that allows you to send your message to a big list all at once.

- Use a "from" email address that identifies your group (i.e. Liberty High Cheerleaders) or a person's name everyone will recognize (i.e. Liberty High Principal Smith) so more people will open the message

- Announce on your social media that the email will be going out and you need everyone's participation

87. Fake Kidnapping

Their ransom pays your bills!

Description: "Kidnap" the leader of an organization, such as a teacher, principal, minister, elected official, sports coach, or other respected person, and hold him or her for "ransom" until enough funds are collected to meet your goal. Return the "kidnapped" person to his or her point of origin in a dramatic presentation.

Estimated Cost:

Levels of Difficulty:

Obtaining Sponsors/Donations	★
Finding a Venue	★
Recruiting Volunteers	★ ★ ★
Preparation	★
Execution	★

Special Materials/Equipment:

☐ Bandit costumes (masks, fake toy guns like squirt guns)

Sponsors/Donations: NA

Possible Venue(s): Your school — consider timing with a big event like a basketball game

Recommended Volunteers: 5-10 people to make a scene and whisk away the victim

Preparation: Let your school administration and security know in advance about the "ransom."

Execution: Have the disguised "kidnappers" burst into the venue and storm the intended target. Announce that he or she is being kidnapped and that the only way to get the person back is to donate money to your organization. Make it clear how long the person will be held and how much money is needed to win his or her release. Wave around a donation canister as the victim is escorted away.

Tip(s):

- Make it very clear that this is a fake kidnapping.

- Pick someone with a sense of humor who will not mind being held "prisoner" for a short period of time.

- Get the participant's permission ahead of time to ensure that there are no problems, but don't tell the participant what day the kidnapping will occur in order to maintain the element of surprise.

Variation(s):

- Convey the "prisoner" to a fake cell and keep him or her there until enough money is raised to pay for a "Get out of Jail" card.

Did You Know? The Muscular Dystrophy Association (MDA) is famous for its "Lock-Up" fundraisers that are held all over the country, all year long. They encourage participants to share photos of themselves behind bars on social media as well as email and call friends and family to "bail them out." See www.mda.org/lockup.

88. Flamingo Flocking

You've been flocked.

Description: Plant a dozen pink flamingos on the front lawn of a residence or outside a business entrance. Hang a letter around the neck of the lead bird explaining that the recipient has been "flocked" for a good cause and that the only way to get the flamingos to "fly away" is to pay or raise a certain amount of money, like $10 per flamingo. Once the money has been collected, the donor chooses the next recipient, and your volunteers relocate the flock to start the process all over.

Estimated Cost:

Levels of Difficulty:

Obtaining Sponsors/Donations	★ ★ ★
Finding a Venue	★
Recruiting Volunteers	★
Preparation	★ ★ ★
Execution	★ ★

Special Materials/Equipment:

☐ At least a dozen pink flamingo lawn ornaments

Sponsors/Donations:

- Approach lawn and garden stores, or discount stores with garden centers for donations of flamingos.

Possible Venue(s): Pick the first "flocking" the location, and let those who have been "flocked" decide where the next landing will be.

Recommended Volunteers: 10+ depending on how many flocks are deployed at one time

Preparation: Brainstorm with your group to decide on the first flocking recipient. Write a short letter explaining how the fundraiser works and give a phone number that the recipient can call once the correct amount of money has been raised.

Execution: Try to set up the birds without being seen, since the element of surprise is part of the fun. Send volunteers to pick up and relocate the birds each time the donation amount has been raised.

Tip(s):

- Have up to six flocks of a dozen birds each circulating to maximize donations.

- If you encounter someone who complains about being "flocked," collect the birds promptly, ask the previous recipient to designate another "victim," and relocate the flock.

Variation(s):

- Allow flocked homeowners options to pay to have the flock removed, pay even more to have them moved to someone else's yard, or pay optional "insurance" against getting flocked again.

Web resource(s):

Yes, you can even order a kit on Amazon.com to make it easy:

https://www.amazon.com/Flamingo-Flocking-Flocked-Corrugated-Plastic-stores/dp/B004KTHBMM

Success Story According to Amazon customer Sasha Parker, the flamingos were "fabulous" for a cheerleading fundraiser. "They are easy as pie," she says, "I am ordering more sets so we can have more 'flocks' for our fundraisers!"

89. Flyer Delivery

This frequent flyer program pays cash.

Description: Offer for your organizations' members to deliver advertising flyers for local businesses. Charge by the piece or by the hour. Since it can be pricey to mail printed pieces, business owners are likely to welcome the opportunity to use your members instead; plus the personal service is a big bonus.

Estimated Cost:

Levels of Difficulty:

Obtaining Sponsors/Donations	★
Finding a Venue	★
Recruiting Volunteers	★
Preparation	★
Execution	★

Special Materials/Equipment:

☐ Bag, preferably emblazoned with your organization's name (to carry the flyers in)

Sponsors/Donations:

• None needed, unless you would like to raise cash to pay for bags in which to carry the flyers. Any company that delivers, from restaurants to newspapers, might be interested in donating funds in exchange for a printed logo on the bag.

Possible Venue(s): Pizza and other restaurants, hair and nail salons, home improvement companies, and candidates running for public office are good options.

Recommended Volunteers: 10+ to deliver flyers

Preparation: Make sure the company you are delivering for has the necessary solicitation permits.

Execution: Pick up the flyers from the client or print shop, divide them among volunteers, drop them off from door to door. Try threading them through the front door handle or inserting them securely into the seam of the door.

Tip(s):

- Send volunteers out in pairs or small groups for safety.

- Do not place flyers in mailboxes, which are considered federal property. The sponsoring organization could be fined if someone complains.

Variation(s):

- Place flyers on car windshields in big parking lots to distribute more flyers in a shorter amount of time.

90. Fundraising by Blogging

Fundraising often starts with "friendraising." Tell your story and they'll want to help you!

BLOG   **Description:** Keeping potential donors and your community informed of your group's current activities is crucial, both to attract donations and to build goodwill among people who are genuinely interested in your cause. A blog can connect readers, build community by encouraging comments and discussions, and more. Use a blog to market the organization, give information about a fundraising campaign in progress, and provide up-to-date news about your activities.

Estimated Cost: ⓢ

Levels of Difficulty:

Obtaining Sponsors/Donations	★
Finding a Venue	★
Recruiting Volunteers	★ ★ ★
Preparation	★ ★ ★
Execution	★ ★ ★

Special Materials/Equipment:

☐ Computer with internet access, live website, blog publishing tool (like wordpress.com)

Sponsors/Donations:

- Form an alliance with another school or community group or local business where your blog can appear, in addition to on your own website. Include a donation button on the site to make it easy for blog readers to donate.

Possible Venue(s): Your organization's own website or that of an affiliated or complementary organization that shares your values is effective.

Recommended Volunteers: 1-2+ who enjoy writing, can write grammatically and logically, and can meet deadlines regularly and reliably

Preparation: Read widely and follow developments in your field to get blogging ideas.

Execution: Establish a set schedule — say, once a week — to blog; then, meet it without fail. A blog that is not updated regularly will not induce readers to return to the website to find out what is new and exciting.

Tip(s):

- Offer PayPal as an easy payment option for donors.

Variation(s):

- Try podcasting valuable information and news that might be attractive to potential donors and include updates about your organization.

- Keeping up a Twitter or Instagram account for your organization is also a great way to get a following and make people aware of ways to participate and donate.

91. Lend a Helping Hand

This will earn your group needed funds, and also a good reputation.

Description: Offer to do odd jobs and simple household tasks in your community for a fee. Tasks might include gardening, weeding, shoveling snow, raking leaves, painting, window cleaning, or dog walking. Charge by the hour ($10 an hour is reasonable) or by the job.

Estimated Cost:

Levels of Difficulty:

Obtaining Sponsors/Donations	NA
Finding a Venue	NA
Recruiting Volunteers	★ ★ ★
Preparation	★ ★ ★
Execution	★ ★ ★ ★ ★

Special Materials/Equipment: NA

Sponsors/Donations:

- Ask the homeowner to provide any necessary materials or equipment.

Possible Venue(s): Virtually all work will be done at the homeowners' homes.

Recommended Volunteers: 10+ so you have a large enough pool of people with varying skills to handle the tasks that will come up

Preparation: Advertise your organization's capabilities and availabilities on social media and hang flyers around the neighborhood. Contact local media because they might be interested in doing a human-interest story on your group.

Execution: Publicize an email address or phone number for people to call to schedule your work group. Have one or two organized members create a work schedule to make sure all jobs are handled promptly. Wear your group's swag when working.

Tip(s):

- Offer both a phone number and an email address at which interested parties can contact your organization.

- Put a link on your organization's website and social media to a page with details about the services you offer.

Variation(s):

- Offer simple computer services like hooking up components and uploading or updating software and printer drivers — this is particularly valuable if you have communities of retirees in your area.

92. Massage-A-Thon

Help donors relax and see how much they give!

Description: Partner with a massage therapist or massage therapy studio to offer everything from chair massages to whole body treatments. Typically, a portion of the proceeds is donated to the charitable organization (usually 30 to 50 percent of the massage cost), while the balance goes to the massage therapist.

Estimated Cost:

Levels of Difficulty:

Obtaining Sponsors/Donations	⭐⭐
Finding a Venue	⭐⭐⭐
Recruiting Volunteers	⭐
Preparation	⭐⭐
Execution	⭐

Special Materials/Equipment:

☐ Massage tables or chairs

Sponsors/Donations:

- First, ask if any of your members' parents are massage therapists.

- A newly-licensed massage therapist might be willing to donate their services to help them find potential clients. However, a popular, well-established massage therapist may be in a better financial situation to help you.

Possible Venue(s): A massage therapy studio, or a private room can be set up with a portable massage table at your school or another community building.

Recommended Volunteers: 3-4 to find a massage therapist and schedule appointments with customers

Preparation: Create an event on social media and ask your members to share and promote the event. Hang flyers where student athletes will see them, and email parents if possible.

Execution: Assist massage therapists with the transport of chairs and tables to the venue, if necessary. Have one or two organized members take reservations and fill up the massage therapist's schedule to maximize their time.

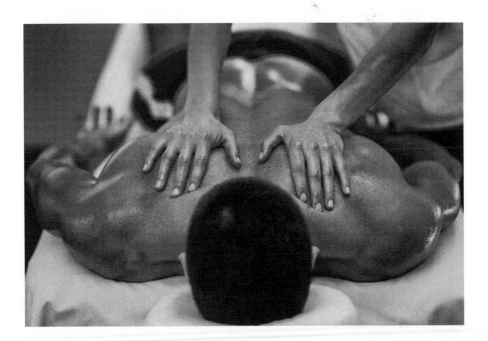

Tip(s):

- Combine with an athletic event, like a 5k, bike ride, or triathlon for a ready-made audience of tired athletes who would enjoy a massage.

93. Peck for a Pig

Because you're already thinking about which teacher you want to see kiss the pig.

Description: Allow students to vote by putting money in the collection jar of the teacher or principal they most want to see have to kiss a pig.

Estimated Cost: $

Levels of Difficulty:

Obtaining Sponsors/Donations	⭐ ⭐ ⭐
Finding a Venue	⭐
Recruiting Volunteers	⭐
Preparation	⭐ ⭐ ⭐
Execution	⭐

Special Materials/Equipment:

☐ Pet pig

☐ Containers to collect cash

Sponsors/Donations:

- Contact local businesses for donations and offer them logo space on your publicity materials. Even if you are able to raise a lot of cash from sponsors, set the bar high for community donations to generate extra excitement.

Possible Venue(s): This challenge is best held as part of another event like a city or church festival or school activity. Collect money during sporting events, so you can use the sports facility or playing field for the kiss.

Recommended Volunteers: 2-3 to find the pig, the potential smoocher, and donors

Preparation: Create a poster or tally board featuring a picture of the pig. Publicize the event in as many free and low-cost publications as possible. Try to recruit a local celebrity like a TV anchor, radio DJ, sports star or coach, or elected official to do the deed. If you land a TV personality, be sure to give the station the exclusive right to report on the story.

Execution: Set up donation containers and coax people to come over and drop in their cash donations. Make a big production out of the pig-kissing payoff after announcing that the donation goal has been met.

Tip(s):

- Keep an eye on the containers to deter theft and remove cash from the containers regularly.

Variation(s):

- Substitute the local school's team mascot for the pig to encourage team spirit.

Success Story   On her blog, a Texas mom writes about her kids' elementary school holding this fundraiser with their family's pet pig, Piper. By bringing in the pig during lunch and having students vote with their donations for which teacher would kiss the pig, they raised $928. Read more and see pictures at **https://pinkunderbelly.com/tag/kiss-a-pig-contest/**

94. "Please Do Not Come" Fundraiser

No event is easier to put on than a nonexistent event.

Description: This event invites supporters not to attend a lavish dinner with superb entertainment and fabulous door prizes — because there actually is no such event planned! Make it clear on the invitation that the event will not actually occur, but invite people to buy tickets anyway to support your cause. Invited guests will get a good laugh and likely will be more than happy to support an event they do not have to attend.

Estimated Cost:

Levels of Difficulty:

Obtaining Sponsors/Donations	★ ★
Finding a Venue	NA
Recruiting Volunteers	★
Preparation	★
Execution	★

Special Materials/Equipment:

☐ Printed invitations, donation cards, envelopes and postage, if mailing invitations

Sponsors/Donations:

• If mailing invitations, ask a print shop to donate the cost of the invitations and other materials.

Possible Venue(s): NA

Recommended Volunteers: 5-10 if designing, printing, and mailing invitations

Preparation: Decide whether you will send old-school printed invitations, send a digital invitation by email, or simply create an event on Facebook. The demographics of your audience will help you decide — to attract older donors, a hand-addressed, mailed invitation may be most effective. To reach parents of your members and a younger crowd, digital invitations are probably just fine.

Execution: Literally, nothing needs to be done once the invitations go out except to wait for donations to roll in.

Tip(s):

- Follow up the invitation with personal emails or phone calls.

Variation(s):

- Hold a "Do Not Come" sporting event like a virtual 5k race.

- Hold a Bakeless Bake Sale, inviting people not to do all the work that goes into it (bake, find a recipe, shop for ingredients, mix, cook, wash dishes, clean up your kitchen, deliver the product, or stand outside and try to sell anything). Instead, they can make a check out to your organization, stay home, and enjoy the free time as they wish.

95. Pool Party

When it gets hot, you'll be the coolest game in town.

Description: This is fun summertime event for any age group. Admit kids for a discounted admission fee. Sell poolside food and snacks and offer carnival-style games with prizes.

Estimated Cost:

Levels of Difficulty:

Obtaining Sponsors/Donations	✪ ✪ ✪
Finding a Venue	✪ ✪ ✪ ✪ ✪
Recruiting Volunteers	✪ ✪ ✪ ✪ (due to safety issues)
Preparation	✪ ✪ ✪ ✪ ✪
Execution	✪ ✪ ✪

Special Materials/Equipment:

☐ Pool toys

☐ Tables or tent (for concession items)

☐ Carnival games (rented or constructed)

Sponsors/Donations:

• Approach toy stores for donations of stuffed animals or other toys that can be awarded as prizes.

- Offer signs and other publicity to pool owners who give permission to use their facility.

- If a membership facility like a fitness center gives you free pool time, offer to hand out membership applications to participants.

- Ask a party rental company to supply some beach chairs and a couple of beach umbrellas.

Possible Venue(s): High schools, YMCA/YWCA, fitness facilities, community centers, and city pools work well.

Recommended Volunteers: 10 to oversee carnival games, prepare and sell food, sell tickets, in addition to a certified lifeguard

Preparation: In addition to advertising the event and promoting it in the media, it will be necessary to make, purchase, or rent carnival games. These may include ring toss, baseball or basketball toss, wheel games, card games, and ticket games. It may be necessary in your state to have a food vendor license if you will be cooking food on site. You also may need a state license to hold a raffle. Search your state government's website for information.

Execution: Set up the carnival activities and food area at a safe distance from the pool. Hold hourly raffle drawings. Keep a close eye on the pool to ensure that everyone is safe.

Tip(s):

- Fill a small plastic pool with ice to keep soft drinks cold.

Variation(s):

- Create your own water day with sprinklers, blow-up water slides, Slip 'n Slides, water balloon tosses, and other fun water games.

96. Read-a-Thon

Reading is pretty much your number one job in school — why not raise money doing it?

Description: The concept is similar to a walkathon that asks donors to pledge money to be paid for every mile walked. Students get family and friends to pledge and the students do the reading. With nothing to sell, and rewards for reading, this is a project even the strictest teachers can support!

Estimated Cost:

Levels of Difficulty:

Obtaining Sponsors/Donations	⭐
Finding a Venue	⭐
Recruiting Volunteers	⭐⭐
Preparation	⭐⭐
Execution	⭐⭐

Special Materials/Equipment: If using an online system like Read-a-Thon.com, they provide online tools and materials, and the only thing needed are books, a place to read, timers, and internet access.

Sponsors/Donations:

- To give your read-a-thon a boost, you could solicit local businesses to sponsor the event and make a donation before it starts. Use the sponsoring business' name throughout the fundraiser, i.e. "Sixth Street School Readathon Sponsored by Acme, Inc."

Possible Venue(s): Many schools allow read-a-thons to take place in the classroom during class, but you could also hold the event anywhere conducive to reading, like a library or community center.

Recommended Volunteers: You will need enough volunteers to time all readers and enter their progress on the website.

Preparation: Follow the guidelines on the company's website. Most recommend you have a leader from your group sign up online, and the company will give you a timeline of when to hang up the posters they provide, and send home supplied flyers with students.

Execution: Readers' own supporters will log in online and make pledges. You will need to have your volunteers time the reading sessions and enter the information on the website.

Tip(s):

- Encourage donors to make a one-time, lump-sum donation. These types of payments are usually easier to collect than pledges.

Web resource(s):

This comprehensive website explains the program in a colorful slideshow. They provide a wealth of instructions, publicity and informational materials, and online donation tools for donors: **www.read-a-thon.com**

Success Story Read-a-Thon's website tells the story of Richland Elementary School, which raised more than $41,000 through their first read-a-thon. The fundraising chairperson says the principal, teachers, students, and parents all loved it, and they raised more than twice as much as any other fundraisers they had tried.

97. Sacrifice Something You Love

Most people will donate the cost of their morning coffee, lunch out, or weekly manicure if you ask.

Description: This simple fundraiser asks your members' families, students at your school, or members of your community to give up something they truly love, and donate the cost of that special treat to your cause instead. It can be a one-time donation or a donation made daily or weekly over a specified period of time. In either case, there is some sacrifice involved, which makes the donation even more valuable.

Estimated Cost:

Levels of Difficulty:

Obtaining Sponsors/Donations	⭐⭐
Finding a Venue	⭐
Recruiting Volunteers	⭐
Preparation	⭐
Execution	⭐

Special Materials/Equipment: NA

Sponsors/Donations:

- In addition to posting on social media, you may want to record a short video in which someone from your group can explain what you are asking donors to do.

Possible Venue(s): NA

Recommended Volunteers: Ask all members to promote to their friends and family and share event information on social media.

Preparation: Publicize the event for a couple weeks before it starts, explaining how the fundraiser works. For example, ask donors to sacrifice the cost of anything from a single latte or fast food meal, to the cost of a nail appointment, a movie ticket, a pizza, and so on. Stress that a contribution of any amount, no matter how small, is welcome. Set up an online donation mechanism like a GoFundMe page and invite donors to also share their stories about how much they are donating and why in short video clips and tagging you on Instagram.

Execution: On the day or days of the event, publicize on social media and ask all your members to share. Ask members to make the first donations themselves and share their videos to help get the ball rolling.

Tip(s):

- Have members solicit their families and get their videos and donations before the event even starts to kick it off successfully.

98. Social Media and Networking Class

What comes naturally to you is like a foreign language to your grandparents.

Description: An exciting event to introduce parents and grandparents to the mysteries of social media and networking that are second nature to their kids. The class can touch on Facebook, Instagram, Twitter, Skype, and texting.

Estimated Cost:

Levels of Difficulty:

Obtaining Sponsors/Donations	★ ★ ★ ★ ★
Finding a Venue	★ ★ ★ ★ ★
Recruiting Volunteers	★ ★ ★ ★ ★
Preparation	★ once the program is up and running
Execution	★ ★ ★

Special Materials/Equipment:

☐ Computer or tablet with Internet access

☐ LCD projector

☐ Handouts detailing what the class covers

Sponsors/Donations:

- If no one in your organization is comfortable teaching the class, ask someone who teaches computer classes to donate his or her time.

- Alternately, contact the IT department of the local university or college and ask for a referral to a gifted student who would be willing to teach.

Possible Venue(s): A classroom at your school, or a church meeting room or community center would work well.

Recommended Volunteers: 3-4 including 1 to teach and 2-3 to set up equipment, collect fees, and pass out handouts

Preparation: Promote the class in community newspapers, in Parent-Teacher Association (PTA) newsletters, on social media, and on your website. Initially, the instructor can create a curriculum for the class that can be taught over and over in the future.

Execution: Set up the equipment, dim the lights, and share your knowledge.

Tip(s):

- Create a second class to cover other types of electronic media like YouTube, LinkedIn, blogs, podcasts, and search engines.

Variation(s):

- Offer tips on how to download music and podcasts from iTunes and add them to an iPod or iPad.

- Demonstrate how to use Google tools like Gmail, Google Alerts, Google Earth, and others.

99. Speaker Forums

A mini-Ted-Talks-type event could be a unique fundraiser for your group.

Description: Invite the most interesting and articulate people in your community, from artists and musicians to authors and government officials, participate in a speaker's forum. Charge an admission fee and give the audience an opportunity to ask questions at the conclusion of the talk.

Estimated Cost:

Levels of Difficulty:

Obtaining Sponsors/Donations	★
Finding a Venue	★ ★ ★
Recruiting Volunteers	★
Preparation	★ ★
Execution	★

Special Materials/Equipment:

☐ Sound equipment

☐ Microphone and stand (consider a miniature clip-on mic for the speaker's convenience and comfort)

☐ Podium

☐ Seating

Sponsors/Donations:

- Approach local business owners to sponsor the event or to cover the cost of refreshments or the venue. Match the sponsors to the speakers; for example, contact a bookstore to sponsor an author. Find a printer willing to print admission tickets.

Possible Venue(s): Your school's auditorium, a community playhouse, or even a library meeting room could be a great option.

Recommended Volunteers: 3-5 to line up speakers, sell tickets, and serve refreshments

Preparation: Choose a theme for the speakers' presentations. Send personal invitations to interesting people in your community. Inform the media about the event, giving information both about the speakers and how to buy tickets. Prepare bios of the speakers that will be read to introduce them. Create an event on social media and invite the entire community.

Execution: Greet the speaker and audience members as they arrive and escort them to a comfortable "green room" where they can relax and prepare. Have water available for them at the podium. Select one member of your group to facilitate the speeches and introduce speakers.

Collect or sell tickets at the door, and have information about your group and the project you're raising money for on a table with a donation jar.

Serve refreshments after the talk. If speakers are willing, invite them to mingle with the audience.

Tip(s):

- Present speakers with a certificate of appreciation.

Variation(s):

- Show interesting educational movies and hold movie forums.

100. Walking Billboard

Are your members dedicated enough to dress like a hot dog or spin a sign to make bank?

Description: Contact a wide variety of businesses and offer to have your members wear the costume of their choice for an hour or two in a public place or spin a sign outside their business. In exchange, they give you a set donation amount per human billboard, like $25 or more.

Estimated Cost:

Levels of Difficulty:

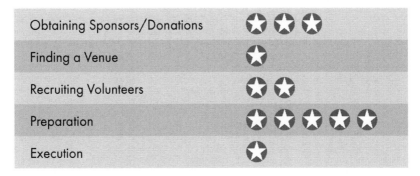

Obtaining Sponsors/Donations	⭐ ⭐ ⭐
Finding a Venue	⭐
Recruiting Volunteers	⭐ ⭐
Preparation	⭐ ⭐ ⭐ ⭐ ⭐
Execution	⭐

Special Materials/Equipment: NA

Sponsors/Donations:

- Any company is a potential candidate for this fundraiser since virtually every company desires more advertising to increase business.

- You may find that small-to-medium size companies will be most interested in participating since they tend to have small or nonexistent advertising budgets.

Possible Venue(s): Malls and shopping centers or anywhere else a lot of people will see the promotions for the donating business.

Recommended Volunteers: 12+ to appeal to businesses regarding advertising exposure

Preparation: Ask your members' parents to help compile a mailing list of local businesses, then send an email offering to walk around advertising for them on a specific date. Call or visit selected business owners. Create a schedule to keep track of the commitments.

Execution: Assign your volunteers to locations and costumes to walk around and get noticed.

Tip(s):

- Make giant sandwich posters to wear to attract extra attention.

101. Writing Letters for Support

An old-fashioned letter gives you plenty of time and space to explain your need for funds.

Description: Make a heartfelt plea for funds by writing a solicitation letter to potential donors. Start with your own friends and family before expanding into the community-at-large. Enclose a donation card indicating several levels of giving, such as $15, $25, $50, and $100. Include an "other" line where donors can fill in the amount of their choice.

Estimated Cost:

Levels of Difficulty:

Obtaining Sponsors/Donations	★ ★
Finding a Venue	NA
Recruiting Volunteers	★ ★ ★ ★ ★
Preparation	★ ★
Execution	★ ★

Special Materials/Equipment:

- ☐ Stationery
- ☐ Stamps

Sponsors/Donations:

- Solicit office supply stores or print shops for donations of stationery.

- Ask a professional fundraiser or another business communicator to help write the letter. Ask people sympathetic to your cause for funds to purchase stamps and provide names for a mailing list.

Possible Venue(s): A location to stuff and address envelopes

Recommended Volunteers: 3-4 to fold and stuff letters and donation cards into envelopes, address envelopes or apply self-stick labels, affix postage, and deliver the envelopes to the post office

Preparation: Compile a mailing list of members' families, friends, and community members who might be inclined to give.

Execution: Print, stuff, and mail the letters.

Tip(s):

- If your organization does not have its own stationery, be sure to purchase high-quality paper.

- Affix stamps on the envelopes rather than using a postage meter to make the solicitations look like business mail rather than junk mail. Pay the cost of return postage to increase the response.

- Keep the letter to one page long. Be sure to explain details of why you're raising money, and give the dollar amount of your goal.

Variation(s):

- Include a small gift, like stickers. When people receive something, they often feel more obliged to give.

Bibliography

Strausbaugh, John. "Coin. Smile. Click!" The New York Times, The New York Times, 13 Mar. 2008, www.nytimes.com/2008/03/14/arts/14expl.html.

Lincoln, Janelle. "Family Portrait Fundraiser." PTO Today, PTO Today, www.ptotoday.com/pto-today-articles/article/789-family-portrait-fundraiser.

Gandhi, Lakshmi. "The Extraordinary Story Of Why A 'Cakewalk' Wasn't Always Easy." NPR, NPR, 23 Dec. 2013, www.npr.org/sections/codeswitch/2013/12/23/256566647/the-extraordinary-story-of-why-a-cakewalk-wasnt-always-easy.

Miller, Alicia. "Cookbook Fundraisers: Recipe for Success." PTO Today, PTO Today, www.ptotoday.com/pto-today-articles/article/70-cookbook-fundraisers-recipe-for-success.

Yeh, Cedric, and Noriko Sanefuji. "Origins of a Fortune Cookie." National Museum of American History, Smithsonian, 5 Aug. 2016, americanhistory.si.edu/blog/2010/07/origins-of-a-fortune-cookie.html.

"Dunking for Dollars! - an Alzheimer's Fundraiser." RCM Senior Living, Retirement Center Management, 12 June 2017, www.rcmseniorliving.com/2017/06/alzheimers-fundraiser/.

"Game Night Fundraiser Exceeds Goals." Zakat Foundation of America, Zakat Foundation of America, 8 Nov. 2015, www.zakat.org/en/a-successful-game-night/.

"Windy City Rubber Ducky Derby." Windy City Rubber Ducky Derby, Great American Merchandise & Events, Aug. 2017, www.duckrace. com/chicago.

Whitler, Larry. "Larry Whitler." Facebook, 2017, www.facebook.com/ 12StringPoet.

Munson, Caleb, and Sarah Curry. "Fundraising at Auburn University." *AIAS*, American Institute of Architecture Students, 28 Nov. 2016, www.aias.org/fundraising-auburn-university/.

"Candle Facts & Figures | NCA." *National Candle Association*, National Candle Association, 2017, candles.org/facts-figures-2/.

Beck, Evelyn. "Magazines: Focus on Renewals, Discount Prices." *PTO Today*, PTO Today, 22 Jan. 2014, www.ptotoday.com/pto-today-articles/article/804-magazines-focus-on-renewals-and-discount-prices.

"Elementary School Fundraiser Exceeds Expectations." Myfundraiser, Mixed Bag Designs, 2016, myfundraiser.mixedbagdesigns.com/ testimonials.

Schwedel, Heather. "Well-Armed: A History of Teen Bracelet Crazes." Racked, Racked, 16 Sept. 2015, www.racked.com/2015/9/16/9331215/ bracelet-teen-trends-rainbow-loom-friendship-bracelets.

"Featured Fundraisers." Phoneraiser, Phoneraiser.com, 2016, www. phoneraiser.com/featured-fundraiser/.

About the Author

Lisa McGinnes is a writer and editor who enjoys exploring the natural world in her kayak and on her mountain bike.

An alumna of Western Michigan University, she studied public relations and journalism. Lisa has experience in print and broadcast journalism, and has worked with several nonprofit organizations as a public relations and fundraising specialist.

She is the author of *So You Want to Be a Fashion Designer* from Atlantic Publishing.

Lisa and her husband love living in Florida, where they can have year-round outdoor adventures.